Simpson, Paul G.
5 SAT critical reading
practice test /
c2011.
3330522 7770
gi   07/21/11

S0-EJO-965

5 SAT
Critical Reading
Practice Tests

Paul G Simpson IV

with the Staff of Test Professors

© Copyright 2011 by Fusion Press

All rights reserved.

No part of this book may be reproduced in any form by photostat, microfilm, xerography, or any other means, or incorporated into any information retrieval system, electronic or mechanical, without the written permission of the copyright owner.

Printed in the United States of America

* SAT is a registered trademark of the College Entrance Examination Board, which was not involved in the production of and does not endorse this book.

All inquiries should be addressed to: www.testprofessors.com

Library of Congress Catalog Card No.: 2011920144

ISBN: 978-0-9796786-5-3

SAT CRITICAL READING PRACTICE TEST 1

Time: 25 Minutes
24 Questions

Directions: Choose the word that best fits the context of the sentence.

1. The rate of ----- in the US remains undercounted due to the official formulas used to calculate the number of those living in indigence.

(A) rapacity (B) veracity   (C) altruism
      (D) impoverishment (E) voracity

2. On the playground and in the halls of schools, expressions of dislike, or even -----, are often explicit and ----- expressions of love.

(A) stinginess…open-handed
(B) discursiveness…shrewd
(C) animosity…defamatory
(D) apathy…spurious
(E) loathing…blatant

3. While the company portrayed its actions in the devastated city as purely -----, it could not shake accusations of selfishness and opportunism.

(A) acquisitive (B) penurious   (C) apropos
      (D) altruistic (E) rapacity

4. Mrs. Affluence is widely known as a -----, who has given millions of dollars to charity and whose altruism has helped countless penurious people.

(A) miser (B) pauper   (C) glutton
      (D) conformist (E) philanthropist

5. The bookstore's customers comprised ----- group, one of heterogeneous backgrounds and disparate tastes.

(A) a ravenous--(B) a digressive--(C) a motley
      (D) a prodigal   (E) an incognito

6. Sancho remained a ----- friend who stood by his friend Don no matter how difficult the hardships that they encountered.

(A) steadfast (B) craven (C) vacuous
      (D) sagacious (E) heterogeneous

7. Any possible deleterious side effects of the new drug cannot be determined by ----- trials; several long-term studies with -----, identical methodologies are required.

(A) baneful…germane
(B) acceding…fawning
(C) mitigating…stout
(D) fugacious…insidious
(E) cursory…uniform

8. Just as the scientist's claims about cloning were proven to be ----- and unlikely, so too were the methods used to arrive at them found to be ----- and riddled with fundamental lapses in the scientific method.

(A) implausible…erroneous
(B) acrimonious…redundant
(C) bleak…transient
(D) esoteric…lackadaisical
(E) articulate…unwarranted

Questions 9-10 are based on the following passage.

She had woken up before the sun, despite the fact that everything had been meticulously prepared for days. She paced and recited the script that she had written for the meeting,
5　making minute adjustments to its language and touching up a tone here and there. Again she wished that she had a family about, perhaps some children and even a husband. But it was only her, the same tired her, in the same ancient
10　apartment, unchanged even by its uncanny tidiness. Before a mirror, she stopped dead to stare at suddenly strange features. Her dark narrow eyes shut out the nose she now thought stubby and the lips she now thought thin. She
15　wondered if she might soon face the same in her half-sister, when the downstairs buzzer called.

9. In line 6, the word "tone" most nearly means

(A) inflection
(B) climate
(C) feeling
(D) style
(E) tint

10. Based on the passage, the woman is primarily waiting for

(A) sunrise
(B) her half-sister
(C) a meeting
(D) her plastic surgeon
(E) her husband and children

Questions 11-12 are based on the following passage.

While the active pursuit of criminals by the police may now drive innumerable television dramas, the investigative functions of the police are a distinctly modern
5　phenomenon. In archaic times, police forces were relied upon exclusively to control crowds. In ancient Greece, for example, police units composed of slaves kept order at large public gatherings. Investigations into any crime fell
10　on the shoulders of the Greek citizens themselves. By the 18th century, German and French police forces were charged with promoting social good and public health but not with any investigative duties. It was not
15　until the early 19th century, with the establishment of the London Metropolitan Police, that a police force acquired the responsibilities of investigation.

11. The primary purpose of the passage is to

(A) elucidate the history of the police
(B) dismiss the necessity for police investigations
(C) accentuate the enduring need for police officers
(D) profile an exemplar of police investigation
(E) trace the origins of police investigation

12. In line 12, the word "charged" most nearly means

(A) entrusted
(B) accused
(C) attributed
(D) saturated
(E) filled

Questions 13-24 are based on the following passages.

Passage 1

The recent substantiation of violence executed by groups of wild chimpanzees made headlines throughout the world. One particular instance, in which a group of males killed and
5   then ate an infant from a neighboring community, garnered particular attention. The obvious question is why, in a media-saturated culture that rarely pays heed to any event in Africa, would an event in Gombe National
10   Park in Tanzania seize such bold-point headlines.

After all, these chimpanzees were feral, and violence in the wild should not be astounding. Perhaps it was, as some have
15   proposed, simply the sensational aspects of the event. Murder, of an infant no less, and cannibalism held the grim fascination of a tabloid story. Possibly, as others have propounded, the event provoked the innate
20   sense of human curiosity which demanded to know the reasons behind the killing.

The latter explanation seems closest to the truth, although for a different reason than that put forth by its proponents. The fact is that
25   biologists could not, despite their best efforts, elucidate any reason for the killing or the subsequent cannibalism. Thus, it dawned upon all of us, that absurd violence might no longer be the sole domain of humans.

30   This realization, in one stroke, brought people uncomfortably near some fundamental truths. While it was widespread knowledge that humans and chimpanzees have approximately 95% of their genes in common, these
35   percentages remained abstract, until the news of the Gombe killing grounded them in reality. If humans and chimpanzees share this dark aspect, alone among all other species, then the question remains: what other aspects do we
40   share?

The answer to this question might be the salvation of the rapidly-disappearing chimpanzees. For their behaviors may yet show how truly human-like they are, and incite the
45   best of humane behavior in us.

Passage 2

Yes, they are shocking and lurid. But recent reports of chimpanzee violence are overblown and responses to them laughable. Pity any person who must endure yet another
50   pseudo-philosophical treatise that pretends to draw conclusions about the human condition based upon the actions of a few maladjusted chimpanzees. Pity the biologists scrambling to cover a random occurrence with some veneer
55   of rationality and justification.

Let's regain some perspective. Certainly, the birth of a domesticated animal with six legs is an event likely to inspire incredulity in any person who has not witnessed the animal. Yet
60   scientists have substantiated thousands of such events throughout history. In contrast, only two cases of chimpanzee inter-group violence directed at infants have ever been documented. And even the reality of these events has been
65   questioned by some dubious biologists.

The fundamental difference between the cases of mutations in livestock and violence among chimpanzees is one of visibility. It remains almost impossible for a six-legged
70   cow to escape the notice of those people immediately around it. As in prior cases, the news inevitably radiates outwards into the surrounding community and beyond. Scientists then follow and explicate the situation with the
75   vague term "mutation".

No doubt, if humans lived among chimpanzees, the same scenario would have already unfolded, and hundreds of instances of chimpanzee infanticide would already have
80   been recorded. As it stands now, however, only a few researchers are ever observing chimpanzees at any one time. Thus, what would otherwise be ordinary has become extraordinary by virtue of the rarity, not of its
85   occurrence, but of its observance. This rarity does not impart any significance upon events with neither reason nor import.

13. The authors of Passage 1 and Passage 2 would most likely agree that

(A) chimpanzee behavior and human behavior may be interrelated
(B) scientists should expend more effort in the study of chimpanzee behavior
(C) mutations are just as common as instances of chimpanzee violence
(D) wild chimpanzees pose a far greater threat than domesticated chimpanzees
(E) biologists cannot fully delineate the causes of violence among chimpanzees

14. The major point of dispute between the authors of Passage 1 and Passage 2 is

(A) the genetic similarity between humans and chimpanzees
(B) the ultimate significance of cases of chimpanzee violence
(C) the validity of the analogy between mutations in livestock and violence among chimpanzees
(D) the phenomenon of violence and cannibalism among chimpanzees
(E) chimpanzees' motivations for perpetrating violence upon members of other groups

15. In line 17, the word "grim" most nearly means

(A) unrelenting
(B) gloomy
(C) ferocious
(D) uninviting
(E) ghastly

16. In lines 14-21, the author primarily implies that

(A) wild chimpanzees are inherently violent
(B) curiosity is a trait that exists among humans and chimpanzees alike
(C) all tabloids reported the story of the chimpanzee violence in Gombe National Park
(D) multiple explications were offered for the incident of chimpanzee violence
(E) only extreme violence provokes a media response

17. In lines 27-29, the author primarily assumes that

(A) chimpanzees engage in ridiculous violence
(B) everyone is aware of the events in Tanzania
(C) cannibalism is practiced by several species
(D) humans can be as violent as chimpanzees
(E) scientists cannot explain violent behavior

18. In line 34, the author of Passage 1 primarily uses the percentage (95%) in order to

(A) account for the pervasive instances of murder among both humans and chimpanzees
(B) reinforce the commonalities between humans and chimpanzees
(C) discredit the abstraction of scientific analyses and calculations
(D) jeer at those who do not know the exact genetic similarity between humans and chimpanzees
(E) corroborate the quickness with which chimpanzees are disappearing from the wild

19. What best describes the structure of lines 46-55?

(A) a thesis followed by examples
(B) a contradiction followed by elucidations
(C) a concession followed by assertions
(D) a narration followed by illustrations
(E) a refutation followed by endorsements

20. In lines 76-80, the author primarily assumes that

(A) mutations do not occur among chimpanzees
(B) the records of scientists observing chimpanzees are unreliable
(C) chimpanzees would act exactly the same if they lived among humans as they do in the wild
(D) chimpanzee infanticide only occurs in the presence of humans
(E) chimpanzees and humans co-exist in some regions of the world

21. In line 87, the word "import" most nearly means

(A) weight
(B) meaning
(C) message
(D) amount
(E) intent

22. The most likely attitude of the author of Passage 2 towards the "researchers" (line 81) is one of

(A) nonchalance
(B) respect
(C) skepticism
(D) bewilderment
(E) derision

23. Which of the following statements would best undermine the comparison made by the author of Passage 2 in lines 56-71?

(A) mutations have a genetic cause
(B) the reports of mutations in livestock are only substantiated in a small percentage of cases
(C) people who have lived near chimpanzees for centuries have never witnessed violence among the chimpanzees
(D) cows are only very rarely born with six legs
(E) domesticated animals do not show violence like that displayed by wild chimpanzees

24. The author of Passage 2 would most likely regard the statements in lines 41-45 as

(A) moderately craven
(B) astonishingly apathetic
(C) hopelessly confounded
(D) blatantly naïve
(E) harshly indignant

END SECTION

Time: 20 Minutes
19 Questions

Directions: Choose the word that best fits the context of the sentence.

---

1. While the politician ----- that she probably did not win the election, she refused to ----- defeat until the last vote was counted.

(A) calculated…mollify
(B) lamented…condone
(C) articulated…expedite
(D) extricated…appease
(E) acknowledged…concede

2. While the formation of the iceberg was -----, taking thousands of years, its catastrophic effect on the misguided ship was -----.

(A) illicit…deleterious
(B) enhanced…methodical
(C) audacious…profound
(D) indefatigable…notorious
(E) glacial…instantaneous

3. While today's automobiles may be safer than those of the past, they certainly are not as ---- and often break down after only a few years.

(A) cursory (B) durable (C) cerebral
    (D) obtuse (E) dauntless

4. Sunny railed against the ----- of the Donut Diet, which proscribed the eating of doughnuts and only doughnuts for every meal.

(A) endurance (B) vacuity (C) valor
    (D) permanency (E) homogeneity

5. In her latest novel, the author relies on an ----- mixture of modern and arcane language.

(A) opaque (B) identical (C) audacious
    (D) eclectic (E) apprehensive

Questions 6-19 are based on the following passage.

Countless movies feature the hormonal
changes of women during pregnancy. While
these scenes are most often played for comic
effect, their prevalence points towards a
5 popular acceptance of the idea of women
changing through pregnancy and childbirth.
The same acceptance holds for mothers. Take
for example the popular expression about and
from mothers, "I have eyes in the back of my
10 head." This oft-repeated testament to
heightened sensory ability has found support in
scientific studies, which have traced these
changes to the effect of hormones on the brain.
    Only recently, however, has some
15 attention begun to shift to the changes that a
father may undergo. The birth of a child seems
to lower the level of testosterone in fathers.
While the exact mechanism for this drop
remains unknown, it could be triggered by
20 minute quantities of hormones from the
newborn. A study of marmoset monkeys found
that the testosterone levels of fathers fell within
just twenty minutes of being introduced to the
scent of their babies. At the same time that
25 testosterone decreases, the levels of the
hormone prolactin increase. Working in
tandem, these hormonal changes in human
fathers seem to raise their attentiveness to their
babies, as well as to augment sympathy.
30   Another piece to the puzzle of the changes
in fathers is vasopressin. This neurochemical
promotes increased activity and
inquisitiveness. The brains of fathers become
more sensitive to vasopressin, and therefore the
35 fathers experience increased motivation and
heightened problem-solving abilities. These
changes enable the father to bond more deeply
with a baby, and may also allow for enhanced
work ability. Paradoxically, at least at first
40 glance, vasopressin also relieves stress levels
and lowers blood pressure. This natural stress
relief might enable fathers everywhere to bond
more closely with their children, as they are
more suited to meet the constant demands of
45 helpless newborns.
    Yet the natural inclination towards
fatherhood, as manifested in chemical and
brain changes, does not guarantee success as a
parent. Instead a lot of hard work and

50 continued learning seem to be the key factors
in the continued development of a father. In
other words, the more time fathers spend with
their children, particularly during their first
three years, the better fathers they become.
55   This idea might seem intuitive, yet society
is structured in such a way as to proscribe, or at
least minimize, the time that fathers can spend
with their children. This situation should be
examined more closely instead of just taken for
60 granted as normal. For the longer the status quo
is maintained, the longer too many children
miss out on the social, psychological,
cognitive, and educational benefits that
involved fathers can provide.

6. In line 7, the phrase "holds for" most nearly means

(A) reserves
(B) obliges
(C) restrains
(D) prevails
(E) gives

7. Based on the passage, which of the following best
illustrates the findings of the "studies" (line 12)?

(A) hormones allow women to have better senses than
     men
(B) the brains of fathers are affected less by hormones
     than the brains of mothers
(C) hormones influence mothers' brains to produce
     enhanced senses
(D) women's sensory ability depends upon hormones
(E) prolactin is responsible for the sharpening of
     mothers' eyesight

8. The author's claim in lines 18-24 would be most undermined by which of the following statements?

(A) large and small amounts of the hormones of newborns lowers the testosterone levels of human males
(B) the testosterone level of marmoset males that are not fathers drops in the presence of newborns
(C) human newborns possess higher levels of hormones than do marmoset newborns
(D) marmoset monkeys father children with multiple partners regardless of their testosterone levels
(E) human fathers are affected more by prolactin than are marmoset fathers

9. The primary purpose of the third paragraph is to

(A) clarify vasopressin and its effects on fathers
(B) emphasize the encompassing neediness of babies
(C) refute the claim that stress relief is the primary function of vasopressin
(D) elucidate the mechanism whereby vasopressin influences the brains of fathers
(E) punctuate the need for fathers to bond with their children

10. In lines 39-45, the author primarily implies that

(A) the absence of vasopressin would leave fathers incapable of bonding with their children
(B) fathers of newborns work harder than do men without children
(C) vasopressin allows newborns to demand constant attention and care
(D) lower blood pressure in fathers causes their levels of stress to drop
(E) anxiety inhibits the development of the relationship between a father and his children

11. In line 44, the word "constant" most nearly means

(A) steadfast
(B) incessant
(C) unvarying
(D) changeless
(E) unswerving

12. In lines 33-39, the author primarily assumes that

(A) motivation impacts the quality of the relationship between a father and his baby
(B) fathers can pass along their work ethic to their children
(C) sensitivity to vasopressin is crucial to the development of fathers' motivation
(D) sharpened problem-solving capabilities allows fathers to increase their income
(E) the birth of a child permanently changes a father's brain

13. According to the passage, vasopressin (line 31) can produce all of the following effects except

(A) sharpened sense of curiosity
(B) increased analytical capabilities
(C) minimized stress levels
(D) heightened sense of sympathy
(E) decreased blood pressure

14. In lines 26-29, the author primarily states that

(A) diminished testosterone levels result in increased levels of prolactin
(B) fathers who pay more attention to their babies have more sympathetic babies
(C) testosterone and prolactin levels impact the behavior of fathers towards their babies
(D) babies demand attentiveness and sympathy from men with hormonal changes
(E) prolactin has no discernible effect unless it is paired with testosterone

15. Lines 46-51 primarily serve to

(A) extend the author's discussion of hormones and their varied effects upon parents
(B) transition to a broader discussion of fathers
(C) anticipate a possible objection and then answer that objection
(D) strengthen an opinion by means of a specific example
(E) summarize the findings discussed throughout the passage

16. In lines 55-58, the author primarily states that

(A) active fathers raise the intelligence and educational levels of their children
(B) the basic structure of society ensures discrimination against men
(C) fathers must work harder during the first three years of their children's lives than during any other time period
(D) children intuitively sense whether their fathers are sufficiently involved
(E) society limits fathers' participation in their children's lives

17. Based on the passage, the author would most likely endorse

(A) mandatory vasopressin injections for new fathers
(B) public service announcements that educate the public about hormones' effects on mothers
(C) laws that enabled fathers to have more flexible work schedules
(D) more scientific studies on the structure of the society of marmoset monkeys
(E) an increase in parenting classes for both parents and non-parents

18. The author's use of the word "seems" (line 16) primarily implies that

(A) Only fathers experience fluctuations in their testosterone levels
(B) the effects of hormones on men is not completely understood
(C) childbirth has a more profound impact on mothers than it does on fathers
(D) the amount that the testosterone levels of fathers decrease varies
(E) the decline of testosterone among new fathers cannot yet be stated as scientific fact

19. The author's attitude can best be described as

(A) indignant
(B) objective
(C) indifferent
(D) critical
(E) perplexed

END SECTION

Time: 25 Minutes
24 Questions

Directions: Choose the word that best fits the context of the sentence.

1. Although Juan was ----- and tremulous in the presence of his intimidating boss, he summoned the ----- to refute the acumen of her latest plan.

(A) surreptitious…castigation
(B) invariable…delineation
(C) apprehensive…temerity
(D) antagonistic…bafflement
(E) disingenuous…mendacity

2. Instead of becoming clearer, the theory became more ---- as the professor continued his lecture.

(A) abiding (B) germane (C) valiant
    (D) opaque   (E) trenchant

3. The ----- crowd, composed of people of disparate ages and races, ----- the speaker's fawning speech and accentuated the need for action over words.

(A) clandestine…hailed
(B) homogeneous…scorned
(C) extraneous…corroborated
(D) insipid…elucidated
(E) motley…dismissed

4. Flaubert consciously cultivated odd speech and ----- mannerisms in order to hide his true self, which he was too ----- to reveal.

(A) eccentric…pusillanimous
(B) fervid…indomitable
(C) lackadaisical…invariable
(D) deviant…obsequious
(E) stalwart…quixotic

5. Gary's childhood encounter with a wombat, though ephemeral, led to his -----, life-long passion for zoology.

(A) eclectic (B) vapid (C) timorous
    (D) intrepid (E) abiding

6. A forty-pound can of chili, while insufficient for some restaurants, is generally ----- enough for private homes.

(A) abiding (B) imperious (C) resolute
    (D) inane   (E) voluminous

Question 7-10 are based on the following passages.

Passage 1

The establishment of the English colony of Jamestown in May, 1607 represents the birth of the American dream. Yes, the early years of the colony marked a time a chaos and nearly
5 unmitigated catastrophe. Starvation was pervasive. Only sixty of the five hundred colonists survived the winter of 1609-1610.

Yet this appalling mortality rate, like so many other statistics, is misleading. It speaks
10 more to the quality of the early settlers, who were mostly unprepared to diligently work towards success. These "gentlemen [and] libertines", in the words of Virginia's governor of the time, preferred bowling in the streets to
15 planting in the fields.

A subsequent shift in the immigrant population, from the gentleman to the common man, reversed the colony's fortune. Arriving empty-handed, industrious and ambitious
20 Britons quickly instigated an economic boom and prospered.

Passage 2

Given the choice between rotting in debtor's prisons in Britain and journeying to the Jamestown colony, many indigent Britons
25 naturally decided to settle in Virginia. In so "choosing", they replaced the oppression of government masters with the oppression of corporate masters, who operated the Virginia Company. The white colonists' seeming
30 freedom, papered over with the promise of wealth, justified the exploitation of their labor. When these colonists were exhausted, victims of a system that manufactured a mortality rate as high as eighty percent, Jamestown turned its
35 avaricious eyes towards Africa and its people.

Taking advantage of a disposable labor force to grow the addictive cash crop of tobacco on land stolen from the Powhatan people, Jamestown represents the birth of the
40 American nightmare.

7. In line 1, the word "establishment" most nearly means

(A) organization
(B) creation
(C) building
(D) legislation
(E) validation

8. The authors of Passage 1 and Passage 2 would most likely agree that

(A) most colonists came to Jamestown under outside compulsion
(B) British colonies were notorious for their high mortality rates
(C) the founding of Jamestown marks an important turning point in American history
(D) members of the upper classes did not represent the ideal settlers
(E) the Jamestown colonists owed their success to the exploitation of others

9. The author of Passage 2 would most likely respond to lines 18-21 by

(A) acclaiming the diligence of the British colonists
(B) challenging the economic success of Jamestown
(C) denouncing the greed of the common colonist
(D) denigrating the ambition of the Virginia Company
(E) pointing out other sources of Jamestown's affluence

10. Lines 32-35 primarily imply that

(A) Jamestown colonists ignored the high mortality rate
(B) the Powhatan accepted the presence of Jamestown
(C) Jamestown colonists all acquired great wealth
(D) Jamestown eventually relied on slave labor
(E) diligence does not always ensure success

Questions 11-17 are based on the following passage.

We are told incessantly that graffiti is a scourge upon the modern city. Millions of dollars in passive technology are expended to fight it, while anti-graffiti units are in place in
5   every major city in order to catch its perpetrators. And perpetrators they are, if they leave behind nothing but a thoughtlessly sprayed-out name or symbol. But those who carefully execute their visions upon the urban
10 landscape should be lauded as artists.

For graffiti art represents the last true intersection between art and the general public. For, while museums serve an admirable purpose, their time investments and price
15 render them inaccessible to most. (If anyone would counter that museums are free, I suggest that they attempt to gain entry into one of these institutions without paying the suggested "donation".) Graffiti art, on the other hand, is
20 free and fast. If a passerby does not enjoy a work, it is easily ignored. If she appreciates the piece, she can view it on her own schedule and terms.

Unlike museum works, graffiti art is
25 intimately bound to the neighborhood in which it appears. Thus these works are not purely aesthetic, but instead a dynamic interaction of the aesthetic and the cultural. For graffiti art reflects and, at the same time, creates a sense
30 of community and kinship. Belonging to no one and everyone at the same time, graffiti art fills an inherent need for community expression, as it did in New York City in the wake of September 11th. In the weeks that
35 followed this tragedy, countless works of graffiti art sprang up to honor the dead. These works served as focal points of community bereavement, memorializing the deceased in a way that no outside, traditional art could
40 achieve.

11. Lines 6-10 primarily serve to

(A) advocate the acceptance of graffiti as an art
(B) delineate the mechanisms of the fight against graffiti
(C) dismiss the notion of vandals as graffiti artists
(D) punctuate the thoughtlessness of graffiti symbols
(E) vindicate the distinction between graffiti vandals and graffiti artists

12. In line 9, the word "execute" most nearly means

(A) effect
(B) administer
(C) enforce
(D) interpret
(E) kill

13. In lines 13-15, the author primarily suggests that

(A) museum artworks are superior to graffiti works
(B) graffiti artists charge their patrons a higher fee than do museums
(C) museum visitors dismiss those who consider graffiti to be art
(D) graffiti displays require far less of an investment than do museum displays
(E) museums remain inapproachable to most members of the public

14. The aside in lines 15-19 primarily serves to

(A) defy the establishment view of art
(B) discredit a possible objection
(C) reinforce the necessity of donations
(D) relate a personal anecdote
(E) criticize an existing practice

15. The structure of the 3rd paragraph can best be characterized as

(A) a contradiction followed by a parody
(B) an assertion followed by a representation
(C) a clarification followed by a panegyric
(D) a rebuttal followed by a chastisement
(E) a criticism followed by a reassessment

16. In lines 30-34, the author primarily asserts that

(A) a sense of community cannot be fostered by
      museums
(B) graffiti art can respond to community grief in a
      fashion unattainable by other art
(C) graffiti art only cultivates kinships following
      tragedies
(D) traditional monuments are too grand to capture the
      spirit of societies
(E) graffiti artists assumed a leading role in their
      respective communities

17. Based on the passage, which of the following
would the author most likely endorse?

(A) A Picasso sculpture in a private collection
(B) A name painted on the side of a subway car
(C) A monument erected in a neighborhood center
(D) A mural painted on a wall of a community center
(E) An Impressionist painting hanging in a museum

Question 18-24 are based on the following passage.

Society demands a college degree in order for a person to have a chance at the middle-class. Yet, even as the job opportunities for those without four-year degrees decline
5 precipitously, college tuition fees skyrocket. With each attendant hike, universities move further from the grasp of those who do not possess the money to pay for the education.

In recent history, the federal government has
10 buttressed those students without the wherewithal to afford to attend college, doing so through loans and grants. For low-income students the primary means of assistance is the Pell Grant, which does not require repayment.
15 In 1990 the grant covered, on average, 76 percent of a student's tuition fee. Today that number stands at less than one-half.

The short-term consequences of this shortfall are significant. In the next decade, an
20 estimated 3.2 million students, who are otherwise qualified, will not attend college because of its cost. At least two-thirds of those who can still scrape by and earn degrees are now burdened by debt. Not only are these
25 obligations pervasive but they are at record highs, with an average of $22,000 owed per student. For those who would argue that these are individual and not societal concerns, I can only wonder. Would these same people follow
30 the same logic if their own children or grandchildren were priced out of kindergarten or elementary school?

As ominous as the immediate repercussions of lost opportunities in higher education loom,
35 the long-term effects are starker, if not quite as measurable. For education impacts the individual and the society in almost every conceivable manner. In thousands of diverse studies over several decades, rising education
40 levels have been shown to raise income, to increase voting rates, to improve health, to increase life expectancy, and to decrease crime levels. With such universal ramifications, we can no longer afford to be complacent in the
45 face of impending disaster.

This pervasive crisis demands a comprehensive and bold answer, one that would make all public institutions of higher education free. To those critics who would
50 decry the cost of implementing such a proposal, I argue that the cost of approximately 80 billion dollars would be more than offset by savings in health care and law enforcement. I remind those cynical of the idea of government
55 intervention that, not so long ago, free high school education was not universal and had to be fought for by citizens. To the sympathetic who would increase federal aid, I must argue that this option is not a solution, however well-
60 intentioned, but merely a postponement of the time in which traditional federal financial aid will fail to bring the worthy into higher education.

18. In the first paragraph, the author primarily suggests that

(A) universities must continue to raise tuition fees
(B) only the middle-class can afford to attend college
(C) education levels affects people's job prospects
(D) those without four-year degrees are unemployed
(E) college education should be universal

19. Lines 15-17 primarily serve to

(A) rebut an aforementioned opposing point of view
(B) elucidate an example with statistics
(C) refute a previously cited opinion
(D) advocate a new position with research studies
(E) illustrate a reason for a previously-discussed phenomenon

20. In line 21, the word "qualified" most nearly means

(A) fit
(B) restricted
(C) modified
(D) certified
(E) dependent

21. In the passage, the author does all of the following <u>EXCEPT</u>

(A) use personal voice
(B) quote an authority
(C) proffer statistics
(D) ask a rhetorical question
(E) cite scientific studies

22. In lines 33-36, the author primarily states that

(A) the impact of education cannot be measured accurately
(B) the negative effects of not graduating from college are as bad in the future as they are in the present
(C) high tuition fees immediately lead to lost chances
(D) the consequences of lower educational levels are durable and pernicious
(E) completion of higher education is more vital than the completion of elementary school or kindergarten

23. Based on the passage, the "critics" (line 49) would oppose the proposal of the "sympathetic" (line 57) primarily because of

(A) the plan's history
(B) the violation citizens' rights
(C) the high expenditures involved
(D) concerns about law enforcement
(E) the time required to implement the plan

24. In the final paragraph, the author primarily

(A) offers an opinion and then gives examples to support that opinion
(B) dismisses a counter argument and then jeers at those who made it
(C) defends a proposal by delineating how it would work
(D) provide examples that debunk myths associated with higher education
(E) anticipates possible objections and then answers those objections

END SECTION

Practice Test 1
Answer Key and Explanations

Section1

1. D
2. E
3. D
4. E
5. C
6. A
7. E
8. A
9. A
10. B
11. E
12. A
13. E
14. B
15. E
16. D
17. B
18. B
19. C
20. C
21. B
22. C
23. C
24. D

Section 2

1. E
2. E
3. B
4. E
5. D
6. D
7. C
8. B
9. A

10. E
11. B
12. A
13. D
14. C
15. B
16. E
17. C
18. E
19. B

Section 3

1. C
2. D
3. E
4. A
5. E
6. E
7. B
8. C
9. E
10. D
11. E
12. A
13. E
14. B
15. B
16. B
17. D
18. C
19. E
20. A
21. B
22. D
23. C
24. E

Finding Your Score

Raw score: Total Number Right – [Total Number Wrong ÷ 4] = _____

Notes: 1) Omissions are not counted towards your raw score
        2) If the total number wrong ÷ 4 ends in .5 or .75, it is rounded up

Critical Reading Scoring Table			
Raw Score	**Scaled Score**	**Raw Score**	**Scaled Score**
67	800	32	540
66	800	31	530
65	800	30	520
64	800	29	520
63	780	28	510
62	770	27	500
61	760	26	500
60	740	25	490
59	730	24	480
58	720	23	470
57	710	22	460
56	700	21	460
55	690	20	450
54	680	19	440
53	670	18	430
52	660	17	430
51	660	16	420
50	650	15	420
49	640	14	400
48	630	13	390
47	630	12	380
46	620	11	370
45	610	10	370
44	610	9	360
43	600	8	350
42	590	7	340
41	590	6	330
40	580	5	320
39	580	4	310
38	570	3	300
37	560	2	280
36	560	1	260
35	550	0	240
34	550	-1	220
33	540	-2	200

Strength and Weakness Review

Go back to the test and circle the questions that you answered incorrectly. This review will allow you to see what answer explanations to study more closely for problem-solving techniques. It will also allow you to see what question types and passage types you need to review more carefully.

	Section 1	Section 2	Section 3
Passage Types			
Aesthetics / Arts			11-17
Biography			
Fiction	9-10		
History	11-12		7-10
Hard Sciences		6-19	
Social Sciences	13-24		18-24
Question Types			
Assumption	17, 20	12	
Attitude / Tone	22	19	
Inference	16, 23, 24	8, 10, 17, 18	9, 10, 13, 17, 18, 23
Literal Comprehension	10, 13, 14	7, 13, 14, 16	8, 11, 16, 19, 22
Main Idea			
Primary Purpose	11	9	
Structure	18, 19	15	14, 15, 21, 24
Word-in-Context	9, 12, 15, 21	6, 11	7, 12, 20

Section 1

1. D (impoverishment: *poor*)

(A) rapacity: *greedy*
(B) veracity: *true*
(C) altruism: *generous*
(E) voracity: *greedy*

2. E (loathing…blatant)
    hate…obvious

(A) stinginess…open-handed
    greedy…generous
(B) discursiveness…shrewd
    irrelevant…smart
(C) animosity…defamatory
    hate...to insult
(D) apathy…spurious
    indifferent…false

3. D (altruistic: *generous*)

(A) acquisitive: *greedy*
(B) penurious: *poor*
(C) apropos: *relevant*
(E) rapacity: *greedy*

4. E (philanthropist: *generous*)

(A) miser: *greedy*
(B) pauper: *poor*
(C) glutton: *greedy*
(D) conformist: *same*

5. C (a motley: *different*)

(A) a ravenous: *greedy*
(B) a digressive: *irrelevant*
(D) a prodigal: *rich*
(E) an incognito: *secretive*

6. A (steadfast: *same*)

(B) craven: *afraid*
(C) vacuous: *stupid*
(D) sagacious: *smart*
(E) heterogeneous: *different*

7. E (cursory…uniform)
    short-lived…same

(A) baneful…germane
    harmful…relevant
(B) acceding…fawning
    obedient…flatter
(C) mitigating…stout
    make better…strong
(D) fugacious…insidious
    short-lived…harmful

8. A (implausible…erroneous)
    not possible…error

(B) acrimonious…redundant
    bitter…repetitive
(C) bleak…transient
    depressed…short-lived
(D) esoteric…lackadaisical
    different…lazy
(E) articulate…unwarranted
    well-spoken…undeserved

9. A (Scope: *Line 6*)
Since the woman is "reciting", the tone must be related to her speaking voice. Only "inflection" fits this idea.

10. B (Scope: *Whole Passage*)
Line 14 references the "half-sister", and implies that she is waiting for her to show up.

11. E (Scope: *Whole Passage*)
The passage recounts the beginning of police investigations, a fact that makes choice (E) the best choice.

12. A (Scope: *Line 12*)
In the passage, "charged" (12) is linked with "social good and public health" (13). Only the word "entrusted" fits this context.

13. E (Scope: *Passage 1 and Passage 2*)
In Passage 1, the author states the idea in lines 24-27. The author of Passage 2 echoes this idea in lines 53-55.

14. B (Scope: *Passage 1 and Passage 2*)
The author of Passage 1 summarizes his conclusions about the violence in lines 27-29 and 37-40. The author of Passage 2 denies that the violence has any meaning at all in lines 82-87.

15. E (Scope: *Line 17*)
The context sentence contains the ideas of "murder" and "tabloid stories", a fact that gives the word "grim" a meaning and feeling of ghastliness.

16. D (Scope: *Lines 14-21*)
These lines discuss two given explanations for the occurrence of violence. The phrases "as some have proposed" (14-15) and "as others have propounded" (18-19) imply that many reasons were given.

17. B (Scope: *Lines 27-29*)
When the author uses the phrase "all of us", he assumes that everyone knows about the instances of violence.

18. B (Scope: *Line 34*)
In the third paragraph, the author is emphasizing the similarities shared by chimpanzees and humans. The percentage is one more example of this commonality.

19. C (Scope: *Lines 46-55*)
The author of Passage 2 begins with a concession ("Yes, they are shocking and lurid") and then follows with a series of assertions ("Pity any person…"; "Pity the biologists…").

20. C (Scope: *Lines 76-80*)
These lines assert that many instances of chimpanzee violence would have been recorded if humans and chimpanzees lived in the same place. This statement assumes that living among humans would not affect or alter the behavior of chimpanzees.

21. B (Scope: *Line 87*)
The context sentence tells us that import must have the same meaning as "significance" (line 86). Thus "meaning" is the best definition in the sentence.

22. C (Scope: *Passage 2 and Line 81*)
Throughout the passage, Author 2 repeatedly expresses her skepticism about scientists and researchers. See lines 53-55 and lines 73-75.

23. C (Scope: *Lines 56-71*)
In these lines, the author asserts that the difference between mutations in livestock and instances of violence among chimpanzees is one of visibility among people. Choice (C) undercuts this argument by having generations of people watching chimpanzees and not seeing any violence.

24. D (Scope: *Lines 41- 45 and Passage 2*)
These lines state that chimpanzees are human-like, as evidenced by senseless violence, and that therefore humans owe the chimpanzees the consideration of commonality. Since the author of Passage 2 believes that the instances of chimpanzee violence have no meaning, she would most likely view these lines not only as unfounded but also as "naïve".

Section 2

1. E (acknowledged…concede)
  admit…give up

(A) calculated…mollify
  figure out…make better
(B) lamented…condone
  mourn…approve
(C) articulated…expedite
  well-spoken…speed up
(D) extricated…appease
  free…make better

2. E (glacial…instantaneous)
  slow…fast

(A) illicit…deleterious
  illegal…harmful
(B) enhanced…methodical
  make large…careful
(C) audacious…profound
  brave…serious
(D) indefatigable…notorious
  tireless…famous(for a bad reason)

3. B (durable: *long-lived*)

(A) cursory: *short-lived*
(C) cerebral: *smart*
(D) obtuse: *stupid*
(E) dauntless: *brave*

4. E (homogeneity: *same*)

(A) endurance: *long-lived*
(B) vacuity: *stupid*
(C) valor: *brave*
(D) permanency: *long-lived*

5. D (eclectic: *different / odd*)

(A) opaque: *unclear*
(B) identical: *same*
(C) audacious: *brave*
(E) apprehensive: *afraid*

6. D (Scope: *Line 7*)

The context sentence continues the idea of the previous sentence ("the same acceptance"). So the phrase "holds for" must also continue the idea of "prevalence" (line 4). Thus "prevails" is the best choice.

7. C (Scope: *Line 12*)

The context sentence refers to "these changes," a phrase that references lines 7-12. Only choice (C) correctly captures the key ideas in these lines, "mothers" and "heightened sensory ability".

8. B (Scope: *Lines 18-24*)

To effectively weaken an argument, the challenge must address the argument's main ideas. Here, the main ideas are marmoset fathers and a drop in testosterone levels. Choice (B) not only addresses these key ideas, but it also weakens them by showing that fatherhood is irrelevant to testosterone levels.

9. A (Scope: *3rd Paragraph*)

Since the scope is the entire paragraph, the correct answer must contain the main ideas of the entire paragraph (the the ones that are mentioned throughout). Since the most-repeated ideas are "vasopressin" and "fathers", the best choice is (A).

10. E (Scope: *Lines 39-45*)

The referenced lines state that fathers bond more closely when relieved from stress. This idea suggests that stress ("anxiety") makes it more difficult ("inhibits") bonding between a father and his child.

11. B (Scope: *Line 44*)

The description of the newborns as "helpless" (line 45) suggests that their needs never end. Meaning "never-ending", "incessant" is the best choice in context.

12. A (Scope: *Lines 33-39*)

"These changes" (lines 36-37) refer back to "increased motivation" and "heightened problem-solving abilities". Since the lines state that the changes affect the father and his child, choice (A) is the best available answer.

13. D (Scope: *3rd Paragraph*)

Choice (A) is found in line 33 ("inquisitiveness"). Choice (B) is found in line 36 ("problem-solving abilities"). Choice (C) is found in line 40 ("relieves stress levels"). Choice (E) is found in line 41 ("lowers blood pressure").

14. C (Scope: *Lines 26-29*)

The phrase "in tandem" ensures that the correct answer must contain both hormones. Since "fathers" and "babies" both appear in context, they must also appear in the correct answer choice.

15. B (Scope: *Lines 46-51*)

The referenced lines transition from a discussion of fathers and hormones to fathers and other factors such as "hard work" (line 49) and "learning" (line 50). Thus (B) is the best choice.

16. E (Scope: *Lines 55-58*)

The key ideas in the context lines are "society", "fathers", and "children". Only choice (E) contains all three main ideas, and thus it is the best answer

17. C (Scope: *Lines Whole Passage*)

In lines 58-64, the author states that a look should be taken at the way society limits the relationship between fathers and their children because the children miss out on important benefits. This argument suggests that the author would be open to the laws described in choice (C).

18. E (Scope: *Line 16*)

The word "seems" implies uncertainty, a situation best described by choice (E).

19. B (Scope: *Whole Passage*)

Throughout the passage, the author adopts a neutral tone in which he describes facts and, in the final paragraph, dispassionately makes a suggestion. This tone can best be described as "objective".

Section 3

1. C (apprehensive…temerity)
afraid…brave

(A) surreptitious…castigation
secretive…to scold
(B) invariable…delineation
same…to explain
(D) antagonistic…bafflement
hate…confused
(E) disingenuous…mendacity
false…lying

2. D (opaque: *unclear*)

(A) abiding: *long-lived*
(B) germane: *relevant*
(C) valiant: *brave*
(E) trenchant: *relevant*

3. E (motley…dismissed)
to flatter…to insult
(A) clandestine…hailed
secretive…to praise
(B) homogenous…scorned
same…to insult
(C) extraneous…corroborated
irrelevant…to argue for
(D) insipid…elucidated
stupid…to explain

4. A (eccentric...pusillanimous)
 different ...afraid

(B) fervid...indomitable
 passionate...brave
(C) lackadaisical...invariable
 indifferent...same
(D) deviant...obsequious
 different...to flatter
(E) stalwart...quixotic
 brave...odd

5. E (abiding: *long-lived*)

(A) eclectic: *different / odd*
(B) vapid: *stupid*
(C) timorous: *afraid*
(D) intrepid: *brave*

6. E (voluminous: *a lot*)

(A) abiding: *long-lived*
(B) imperious: *strong*
(C) resolute: *brave*
(D) inane: *stupid*

7. B (Scope: *Line 1*)
Only "creation" fits the idea of a new beginning as further emphasized by the word "birth" in line 2.

8. C (Scope: *Passage 1 and Passage 2*)
Passage 1 mentions the idea in lines 2-3, while Passage 2 references it in lines 39-40.

9. E (Scope: *Lines 18-21 and Passage 2*)
The idea of choice (E) points towards passage two's discussion of slavery and its role in Jamestown's economy in lines 34-40.

10. D (Scope: *Lines 32-35*)
The lines reference greed ("avaricious"), as well as Africa and its people.

11. E (Scope: *Lines 6-10*)
"Artists" are referred to in line 10, while the term "perpetrators" in line 6 suggests a hint of criminality captured by "vandals".

12. A (Scope: *Line 9*)
In context, "execute" has a meaning similar to "produce". Only "effect" captures this idea.

13. E (Scope: *Lines 13-15*)
Only this choice contains the two key ideas of the lines: "museums" and "accessibility".

14. B (Scope: *Lines 15-19*)
The phrase "If anyone would counter..." suggests a disagreement that the author then addresses.

15. B (Scope: *Paragraph 3*)
In the 3rd paragraph, the author makes a claim, "graffiti art is intimately bound to the neighborhood in which it appears", and then supports it with an example.

16. B (Scope: *Lines 30-34*)
This choice addresses the key idea of the lines: "community bereavement (grief)" in lines 37-38.

17. D (Scope: *Whole Passage*)
Since the author repeatedly focuses on the idea of communities in the passage, the best choice is (D).

18. C (Scope: *1st Paragraph*)

In lines 3-5, the author states that job opportunities for those without a college education continue to drop significantly. This idea implies that education and job prospects are related.

19. E (Scope: *Lines 15-17*)

The referenced lines provide one explanation for the phenomenon of fewer people being able to pay for college (lines 6-8).

20. A (Scope: *Line 21*)

The author states that money is the only obstacle to students who are otherwise "qualified" to attend college. In this context, only "fit" ("prepared for") makes sense.

21. B (Scope: *Whole Passage*)

Choice (A) occurs in the last paragraph ("I"). Choice (C) occurs in lines 15, 20, and 26. Choice (D) can be found in lines 29-32. Choice (E) occurs in lines 38-43.

22. D (Scope: *Lines 33-36*)

In line 35 the author states that the long-term effects are stark, a term that is further explained by the lines that follow. In these lines are the ideas of the effects being "durable" (lasting a long time) and "pernicious" (exceedingly harmful).

23. C (Scope: *5th Paragraph*)

Since the "critics" are shown to be primarily concerned with cost (lines 49-50), they would most likely raise the same objection to the proposal of the "sympathetic".

24. E (Scope: *5th Paragraph*)

After the author makes a proposal (lines 46-49), she then supports her argument by including opposing viewpoints and then responding to these viewpoints (lines 49-63).

SAT CRITICAL READING PRACTICE TEST 2

Time: 25 Minutes
24 Questions

Directions: Choose the word that best fits the context of the sentence.

1. Her meek appearance and soft-spoken manner belied a domineering and ----- personality.

(A) indulgent (B) indomitable (C) unceasing
    (D) eclectic (E) stalwart

2. While he had a reputation for ---- around strangers, no one thought he was so ----- as to move to a deserted island to avoid them.

(A) homogeneity…incredulous
(B) rancor…zealous
(C) timidity…timorous
(D) temerity…insipid
(E) amalgamation…apprehensive

3. The bank's safe was so ----- that the thieves could not bust it open even with explosives.

(A) conventional (B) vapid (C) acquiescent
    (D) robust   (E) voluminous

4. The businesswoman exploited his ----- and yielding personality in order to gain control of the computer company.

(A) inexorable (B) pertinent (C) vapid
    (D) acceding   (E) invincible

5. The doctor warned that sticking silverware into light sockets while standing in water may be ----- to one's health.

(A) detrimental (B) nonchalant (C) vapid
    (D) insuperable (E) acquiescent

6. The answer to this question is so obvious and ----- that you can guess it before finishing the sentence.

(A) dubious   (B) meticulous   (C) benevolent
        (D) trite   (E) affluent

7. In the interests of national security, the federal government ----- carried out its psychic pet program at a secret and ----- location.

(A) cogently…immaterial
(B) stealthily…timorous
(C) covertly…clandestine
(D) shrewdly…cajoling
(E) blatantly…defamatory

8. The housing advocate reiterated the idea that the city's statistics were -----, disparate from the true facts, and that they were neither ----- nor cogent.

(A) stalwart…inscrutable
(B) indistinguishable…motley
(C) derisive…obtuse
(D) discrepant…salient
(E) dubious…indomitable

Questions 9-12 are based on the following passages.

Passage 1

     The root of emotions lies not in the heart but in the hormone. The arena for an accurate comprehension of emotions is not in the subjectivity of poetry but in the objectivity of
5 laboratories. Take the hormones produced by the thyroid gland. If the hormones are at normal levels, then emotions are stable. If these hormones are overly present, however, they produce a profusion of emotions: anxiety,
10 irritability, and depression. In some cases, a person with an overactive thyroid loses control of emotions altogether, laughing uncontrollably when angry or crying wildly when happy. If a dearth of thyroid hormones exists, it leads to a
15 general dulling of emotions and depression. This small example points to the dominion of hormones over emotions. This universal causal effect must continue to be elucidated by science, without denying individuals their
20 unique experience of the emotions engendered by hormones.

Passage 2

     Those proponents of emotional reductionism, in which each emotion can be correlated to a chemical, conveniently gloss
25 over an important contradiction. Scientists can measure levels of hormones and neurotransmitters with astounding accuracy and precision. Yet these results cannot stand alone. The analytical reports must travel
30 beyond the laboratory door in order to be correlated with the emotions of an individual human being. These correlations are almost never executed with the actual person, a meeting that would shatter the scientific façade
35 of the endeavor. Instead the papers from the lab are correlated with papers based on prior interviews with the person. Yet, even a furtive glance at the questions used to compile the emotional state of the person involved, reveal
40 their radical subjectivity. "Are *you* unhappy more than three days a week?" "How do *you* feel?" I feel that science will never succeed in eradicating the human source of emotion.

9. The authors of Passage 1 and Passage 2 would most likely agree that

(A) subjectivity is an element of emotion
(B) hormones are the root reason for emotions
(C) scientists must continue to correlate the
     objective and the subjective
(D) thyroid conditions pose a serious health risk
(E) emotions are experienced by humans and
     animals

10. The most fundamental disagreement between the authors of Passage 1 and Passage 2 is

(A) the precision with which scientists can measure
     hormones
(B) the cause of emotions within individuals
(C) the validity of subjective questions in
     ascertaining emotional states
(D) the severity of the symptoms that can be
     engendered by hormonal imbalances
(E) the approach that scientists employ in their
     laboratory testing

11. In line 33, the word "executed" most nearly means

(A) run
(B) extinguished
(C) created
(D) legitimized
(E) performed

12. Unlike the author of Passage 1, the author of Passage 2

(A) cites an authority
(B) proposes a solution
(C) employs rhetorical questions
(D) utilizes personal voice
(E) makes an assertion

Questions 13-19 are based on the following passage.

The 1790s witnessed an explosion of the discussion of rights, in the midst of the French Revolution and its unprecedented contention that "Men are born and remain free and equal
5 in rights. Social distinctions can be founded only on the common utility." While this declaration included all men, and not just French men, it did not address the situation of either French women or women as a whole.
10   In 1791, Olympe de Gouges made an audacious attempt to extend the founding principles of the revolution to women. First emulating the language of the declaration in her work, she flatly states that "Woman is born
15 free and lives equal to man in her rights. Social distinctions can be based only on the common utility." While these assertions may seem commonplace today, they were radical and unparalleled in recorded history. She then
20 continues on, in a series of sixteen further articles, to elucidate the equal rights of women in property, security, employment, domestic affairs, politics, and law. Olympe de Gouges argued for these rights without reservation,
25 regardless of a woman's class or social status. Not surprisingly, her *Declaration of the Rights of Women and Citizens* earned her immediate and persistent scorn. Contempt and contumely dogged her into disillusionment with the
30 French Revolution. Following her beheading just two years after the publication of her *Declaration*, de Gouge's "crime" was succinctly summarized by a newspaper account: "She wanted to be a man."
35   Just a year before, Mary Wollstonecraft's *Vindication of the Rights of Woman* had appeared in Britain. In it, she endorses the moral equality of men and women. To uplift and fulfill the moral rights of women, she
40 argues that women must be given the chance to cultivate their rational faculties. To accomplish this end, she advocates the equal education of men and women, not only in substance and scope but also in co-educational facilities. In
45 stark contrast to the reception of de Gouge's work, that of Wollstonecraft was reviewed positively upon its publication. Perhaps the source of its acceptance lie in the essential conservatism upon which the book rests. For,
50 while Wollstonecraft proposes many radical changes in the rights of women, she explicitly calls on men, rather than women, to instigate these changes.

13. In lines 11-17, de Gouges primarily does which of the following?

(A) She calls for equal rights for French men.
(B) She demands a formulation of common utility.
(C) She mimics the language of the Revolution to endorse the absolute equality of women.
(D) She declares the abolishment of all social distinctions in France.
(E) She asserts the equality of women in political and domestic matters.

14. In lines 17-19, the author primarily implies that

(A) de Gouge was addressing a modern audience that could more easily understand her
(B) men cannot fully appreciate the ideas advocated by de Gouge
(C) 18th-century French women took de Gouge's *Declaration* for granted
(D) modern people might not truly appreciate the unconventional nature of de Gouge's work
(E) a woman's respective social status affects her reception of de Gouge's ideas

15. Lines 28-30 primarily imply that

(A) women and men scorned de Gouge equally for her audacity
(B) the French Revolution did not incorporate the idea of equal rights for women
(C) newspapers were primarily responsible for the harsh treatment of de Gouge and of her ideas
(D) the *Declaration* provoked suspicion among men throughout Europe
(E) de Gouge's ideas set the French Revolution upon a new path

16. Based on the passage, the author primarily places the word "crime" (line 32) in quotation marks in order to

(A) encourage readers to think about the nature of crime and its varied punishments
(B) highlight the connection between de Gouge's *Declaration* and her subsequent execution
(C) denounce the penal code in place during the French Revolution
(D) point out the language used to describe de Gouge in the press accounts of the time
(E) suggest that de Gouge's primary offense was not legal in nature

17. In line 41, the word "cultivate" most nearly means

(A) breed
(B) nurture
(C) culture
(D) till
(E) make friends with

18. In lines 49-53, the author primarily states that

(A) Wollstonecraft principally appealed to men in her demands for women's rights
(B) Wollstonecraft demanded that the men of her era fundamentally change
(C) women in 18th-century Britain were more conservative than those in France
(D) Wollstonecraft demanded only limited changes in the rights of women
(E) men treated Wollstonecraft more equally than they treated de Gouge

19. Based on the passage, de Gouge's attitude towards Wollstonecraft would most likely be

(A) awestruck
(B) spiteful
(C) ingratiating
(D) skeptical
(E) disingenuous

Questions 20-24 are based on the following passage.

Recently a controversy erupted when a small school district in the Midwest adopted a new history textbook. Its more than 600 pages contained the minute revision that Abraham
5　Lincoln was "born in" but did not "grow up in" a log cabin. While many people might dismiss this amendment as trivial, it aroused a fervor that highlights a vital debate about the teaching of history to children.
10　　On one side stand the traditionalists, those who are willing to brook historical inaccuracies and omissions. In the Lincoln controversy, they concede that he was not raised in a log cabin, having left his birthplace at the age of seven.
15　Yet they dismiss this imprecision as an innocuous legend that holds an important place in a greater truth, the fact that Lincoln did overcome formidable odds and the poverty symbolized by the log cabin to become an
20　indisputably great president. They advocate this narrative, the rise to success from humble beginnings, as a quintessential example of the American spirit. In this justification, whether implicitly or explicitly, the traditionalists
25　subscribe to a view that children are best served by a curriculum that forms a social and national identity. In short, the truth of the American identity as embodied in the story of Lincoln's upbringing supersedes its historical
30　particulars.
　　On the other side stand the factualists, who regard precision as the hallmark of a solid education in history. Several have weighed in on the Lincoln debate, denouncing the previous
35　"white lie" foisted upon unwitting children and lauding the revision for its integrity. They further underscore the idea that Lincoln's story does not necessitate any embellishment. In fact, they contend that the historical truth,
40　though more intricate than the log cabin narrative, actually adds to the inspirational element of Lincoln's life by giving children a deeper understanding of the severity of the obstacles that he transcended. And, if a
45　particular child finds Lincoln's life drab or lackluster, then so be it. This reaction shows an independent mind, a success in a history curriculum's true objective: teaching children how to think for themselves.

20. The primary purpose of the passage is to

(A) delineate opposing approaches to the teaching of elementary history
(B) denounce recent revisions to textbooks regarding Lincoln's life
(C) advocate a traditionalist approach to the instruction of children in history
(D) accentuate the importance of the development of independent thinking skills in children
(E) profile a comprehensive approach to the teaching of Lincoln's biography

21. Based on the passage, the author most likely uses the phrase "more than 600 pages" (line 3) in order to

(A) laud the diligence of the textbook author
(B) point out the high expectations of the involved school district
(C) underscore the diminutive nature of the revision
(D) decry the wordiness of elementary school texts
(E) dispute the veracity of the textbook's revision

22. Which of the following scenarios is most similar to that described in lines 20-23?

(A) The daughter of a powerful politician who forges a successful career as an actress.
(B) A wealthy businesswoman who declares bankruptcy and then rebuilds her business.
(C) A first-generation immigrant who graduates from medical school is elected Surgeon General.
(D) A son who inherits the family business and runs it profitably for 30 years.
(E) A third-generation corporate lawyer who is elected president after a Senate career.

23. In line 24, the word "implicitly" most nearly means

(A) tacitly
(B) inherently
(C) unconditionally
(D) virtually
(E) unhesitatingly

24. According to the passage, the attitude of the
"traditionalists" (line 10) towards the "people"
(line 6) would most likely be one of

(A) unmitigated animosity
(B) fair appreciation
(C) immeasurable respect
(D) marked cynicism
(E) measured adulation

END SECTION

Time: 20 Minutes
19 Questions

Directions: Choose the word that best fits the context of the sentence.

1. Corn tariffs, which the diplomat had dismissed as ----- issue, turned out to be pertinent and ----- in the negotiations for a new trade agreement.

(A) an apt…pusillanimous
(B) an aberrant…indomitable
(C) a tangential…trenchant
(D) a homogeneous…quizzical
(E) an ingenious…acclaimed

2. In the interests of national security, the federal government ----- carried out its psychic pet program at a secret and ----- location.

(A) cogently…immaterial
(B) stealthily…timorous
(C) covertly…clandestine
(D) shrewdly…cajoling
(E) blatantly…defamatory

3. Faced with the loss of his favorite pet goldfish, Tim's brother was depressed and -----.

(A) meticulous (B) despondent (C) vigorous
    (D) dubious   (E) reclusive

4. Reading over the question, she soon realized that most of its words were -----; she didn't need them to find the correct answer.

(A) precocious   (B) languid   (C) extraneous
    (D) succinct   (E) concurring

5. In the United States, the ----- between the rich and the poor is growing, with the gap widening yearly.

(A) penury (B) disparity (C) amelioration
    (D) brevity (E) languidness

Questions 6-19 are based on the following passage.

When I was in third-grade, I helped to bake a dozen cupcakes for my father's birthday. Once my mother had frosted them and set them aside, I remember staring at them
5   longingly. I pestered my mother to hand one over. I lunged towards the counter before my mother's voice stopped me short. In the moment, I couldn't remember ever wanting anything more. Finally, she told me to think of
10   the cupcakes as a present that could only be unwrapped the following day. Then she added that, if I could stop myself from eating a cupcake that night, I could have two cupcakes in the morning. After she left the kitchen, I
15   remember staring strong up at the counter. But, with great effort, I eventually succeeded in the task of turning the cupcakes into individually-wrapped, inaccessible presents.

What neither my mother nor I knew at the
20   time was that she had invited me to practice metacognition, or the ability to think about thinking. In other words, I had to think about my first thought (wanting the cupcake) in order to avoid thinking about the cupcakes as
25   delicious treats. Only with this avoidance was I able to evade the temptation to immediately eat the cupcake; or, in the scientific terms I now think in, only with avoidance was I able to delay gratification through self-control.

30   A person's self-control can be measured as early as four years of age. Research has shown that the level of self-control among preschoolers can have potent predictive powers. Four-year-olds with less self-control
35   later displayed more bare abilities to cope with stress and problems. In high-school, they found it more problematic to pay attention and build friendships. Those who could delay their gratification longer, on the other hand, earned
40   higher G.P.A.s in high-school and scored significantly higher on the SATs. The disparity in academic success between low delayers and high delayers might be explained, for example, by the latter's ability to study or complete
45   homework even when they really want to watch television or go online. As adults, these same children showed marked differences. The low delayers had more instances of drug addiction, alcohol abuse, and obesity.

50   No doubt, a genetic component exists in whether or not someone can more naturally exercise self-control. However, it remains unclear at this time, what genes or hive of genes may take part in this ability. In the end, it
55   may not matter much. For the intriguing findings about self-control suggest that it can, at least to some extent, be taught. Much as my mother passed onto me the trick of thinking about the cupcakes differently, the mechanisms
60   for avoiding tempting thoughts can be transmitted and learned. Even young children with no real self-control can delay their gratification by thinking about the object of their desire as a picture or distracting
65   themselves from the object through singing.

Knowing the robust effects of gratification delay on academic success, some researchers have proposed that it be taught explicitly in schools. In fact, some schools have attempted
70   to implement these ideas formally, at least on a limited basis. These efforts should be encouraged but with the caveat that their effectiveness will be limited unless the tricks of delay gratification can be cultivated into habit.

6. The first paragraph primarily serves to

(A) clarify a childhood memory
(B) broach a topic with an anecdote
(C) elicit nostalgia for an earlier era
(D) affront the memory of the author's mother
(E) perpetuate a common myth

7. Based on the passage, "the task of turning the cupcakes into individually-wrapped, inaccessible presents" (line 16-18) can best be described as

(A) gratification delay
(B) academic success
(C) genetic component
(D) avoidance
(E) metacognition

8. In line 35, the word "bare" most nearly means

(A) simple
(B) scanty
(C) unembellished
(D) desolate
(E) marginal

9. Based on the passage, which of the following examples best illustrates the idea of "metacognition" (line 21)?

(A) a high-school student who has a high G.P.A and scores well on the SAT
(B) a hungry child who waits to eat dinner until his mother returns home
(C) an adult who is not obese and has no addictions
(D) a middle-school student who always completes her homework
(E) a four-year-old who wonders about why she is thinking about watching television

10. In line 47, the word "marked" most nearly means

(A) pronounced
(B) branded
(C) graded
(D) commemorated
(E) scarred

11. In lines 31-34, the author primarily states that

(A) preschoolers with little self-control will not achieve in high school
(B) young children are incapable of metacognition
(C) the level of self-control in four-year-olds stems primarily from their genes
(D) preschoolers should receive training in order to practice better gratification delay
(E) self-control levels in four-year-olds may prognosticate aspects of their futures

12. The author's tone in the passage can best be described as one of

(A) passive apprehension
(B) awed appreciation
(C) perplexed irony
(D) measured objectivity
(E) general indifference

13. The primary purpose of lines 44-46 is to

(A) undermine an opposing viewpoint
(B) support a thesis with a series of examples
(C) provide a possible reason for a phenomenon
(D) debunk a common myth
(E) accentuate a previously made contention

14. In lines 50-55, the author primarily implies that

(A) scientists have given up looking for the genes that might play a role in self-control
(B) isolating one of the factors of self-control is not as important as utilizing already known factors
(C) learning can override people's natural genetic tendencies
(D) drug addiction has a genetic component that determines a person's self-control
(E) geneticists are not competent enough to distinguish between genes and hives of genes

15. In lines 61-65 the author primarily states that

(A) the level of self-control in young children is genetically determined
(B) parents should instruct young children to distract themselves with singing
(C) young children can acquire skills that allow them to delay gratification
(D) academic success depends solely on gratification delay
(E) young children's self control improves more when they picture objects than when they sing

16. Which of the following, if true, would most undermine the author's statement in lines 31-34?

(A) the levels of self-restraint among high-school students is higher than that among four-year-olds
(B) the self-control tests are actually a measure of intelligence rather than self-control
(C) the desire for a cupcake cannot be compared to the desire to do well in school
(D) new studies show that self-control can now be measured as early as three years of age
(E) four-year-olds cannot understand the self-control tests performed on them

17. In lines 57-61 the author primarily implies that

(A) distraction is the preferred method for delaying gratification
(B) thinking about cupcakes in a different fashion is an important skill
(C) mothers should pass down their knowledge to their children so that they have an advantage
(D) temptation is best avoided among those who have learned gratification delay in school
(E) the author's mother had herself learned metacognition

18. Based on the passage, the author's attitude towards the "schools" (line 69) is most likely one of

(A) extreme indignation
(B) awed reverence
(C) cautious optimism
(D) quiet bafflement
(E) aloof detachment

19. In lines 46-49 the author primarily implies that

(A) high delayers do not suffer from problems such as obesity and addiction
(B) the ability to delay gratification in children foreshadows their lives as adults
(C) genes determine the differences in adults' lives
(D) low delayers cannot practice metacognition
(E) the inability to delay gratification can lead to addictions

END SECTION

Time: 25 Minutes
24 Questions

Directions: Choose the word that best fits the context of the sentence.

---

1. Pitt preferred ----- writing, short and full of meaning, to long and ----- discourse.

(A) enigmatic…ephemeral
(B) disinterested…tangential
(C) pithy…rambling
(D) cursory…steadfast
(E) abiding…fatuous

2. Although the quote is often ----- to Snoop Dog, it was, in fact, originally said by Ghengis Khan.

(A) allayed (B) precluded   (C) attributed
    (D) concurred (E) inundated

3. While Sir Bob is certainly not as ----- as as the indomitable knights of old, he is surely more ----- than the average chicken of today.

(Λ) indubitable…jeering
(B) applicable…stealthy
(C) dauntless…audacious
(D) inane…pervasive
(E) jaded…listless

4. Though their house color ----- only slightly from those allowed by block rules, the Smiths were berated for breaking the color ----- of the block.

(A) touted…discrepancy
(B) denigrated…uniformity
(C) contradicted…eclecticism
(D) digressed…nonchalance
(E) deviated…homogeneity

5. Brian wants to ----- his vocabulary, so he spends eighteen hours each day reading the dictionary.

(A) vacillate (B) augment (C) preclude
    (D) concur   (E) allay

6. In contrast to her colleague's longwinded response, she provided a concise and ----- answer.

(A) astute (B) precocious   (C) succinct
    (D) scanty   (E) extraneous

Questions 7-10 are based on the following passage.

Passage 1

The true historical legacy of Charles Lindbergh rests upon his astonishing non-stop, solo flight from New York City to Paris in May 1927. It is hard to overestimate the fanfare that
5 followed this first successful trans-Atlantic flight, which garnered him several national awards and a ticker-tape parade down Fifth Avenue. Yet the consequences of the "Lindbergh craze", as one contemporary
10 dubbed it, were of far more import. The man himself pioneered new aviation routes and flying techniques that laid the foundation for the modern system of global air travel. Perhaps more importantly, his achievements as an
15 aviation ace won over a public that was, at best, still dubious about the airplane as a viable form of transportation.

Passage 2

When one is labeled as a Nazi sympathizer, particularly by a figure of such
20 moment as FDR, history judges one harshly. Charles Lindbergh will stand forever guilty of bolstering the Nazi war effort by advocating the pacifism of Britain and France in the face of Nazi aggression in 1938. While some
25 historians contend that Lindbergh's first-hand reports of overwhelming German air superiority were fundamentally accurate, the majority assert that these memos allowed the German air force and its planes the time to
30 participate in the devastation of Eastern Europe. It is these dark machines that shall forever overshadow *The Spirit of St. Louis* and its trans-Atlantic triumph.

7. Both passages are primarily concerned with

(A) the aviation achievements of Charles Lindbergh
(B) Lindbergh's role in the globalization of air travel
(C) opinions of Lindbergh held by contemporaries
(D) Lindbergh's participation in World War II
(E) historical judgments of Lindbergh and his deeds

8. The primary purpose of Passage 2 is to

(A) elucidate the circumstances surrounding Lindbergh's trip to Germany
(B) dispute the significance of Lindbergh's accomplishments in aviation
(C) justify a particular historical view of Lindbergh
(D) underscore the harsh reactions of FDR towards Lindbergh and his support of non-intervention
(E) endorse Lindbergh's assessment of the superiority of the German air force in 1938

9. The author of Passage 2 would most likely view the "'Lindbergh craze'" (line 9) as

(A) an inevitable byproduct of the atmosphere of World War II
(B) a justified celebration later eclipsed by an inexcusable act
(C) a lasting phenomenon that deserves its continued prominence
(D) an appropriate response that resulted in the popularization of aviation
(E) a hysterical reaction to an event that was ultimately insignificant

10. In line 20, the word "moment" most nearly means

(A) presence
(B) force
(C) motion
(D) importance
(E) instant

Questions 11-24 are based on the following passages.

Passage 1

The promise of the organic-food industry lies in its reconciliation of environmental responsibility and consumerism. With each purchase of organic food, consumers vote for
5   change. If each dollar represents a vote for more environmentally-friendly farming, then more than thirty billion votes are cast annually. These numbers send a clear message of the demand for the expansion of organic farming
10   and its benefits.

A central tenet of organic farming is the drastic restriction of the employment of synthetic pesticides and fertilizers. The utilization of only natural pesticides reduces
15   the amount of harmful chemicals introduced into the environment. These proven toxins contaminate the local soil, often for years or longer. At the same time, they pose a threat to water supplies. For if the pesticides trickle into
20   ground water sources, or are washed away into streams, they have the potential contaminate water supplies. This latter danger is particularly ominous in the case of artificial fertilizers, which are more prone than pesticides to be
25   washed away by heavy rain and travel into sources of drinking water. The same processes of erosion occur, of course, with natural pesticides and fertilizers. Since these products already exist in the environment, however, they
30   do not pose a hazard to the local environment or its residents.

A more pervasive advantage of organic farming lies in its reduced energy consumption. The limited use of synthetic pesticides and
35   fertilizers redeems the significant energy involved in their production. In addition, energy is saved by nullifying the need for the transportation of these materials, which often travel thousands of miles to reach their final
40   destination. One study has shown that organic farming reduces total energy expenditure by thirty-five percent compared to conventional farming techniques.

The benefits of organic farming, which
45   consumers are increasingly vindicating with their wallets, are destined to propel it from a "fringe" practice and into the mainstream.

Passage 2

While I do not doubt the sincerity of those willing to pay inflated prices for the products
50   of organic farming, I am dubious about the claims of its most ardent proponents. Even disregarding the fact that those who make the most audacious claims often stand to gain the most profit, serious flaws exist in the basic
55   premises of the benefits of organic farming. Energy consumption on organic farms is not diminished but rather enhanced. Though the production and transport energy of artificial pesticides is saved by adhering to organic
60   practices, the subsequent increase in weeds negates this benefit. For these weeds, which are detrimental to crops, are controlled by plowing, the machines for which burn fossil fuels. Furthermore, only twenty percent of all the
65   energy use associated with food production actually occurs on the farm. The rest of the total costs, which organic farming does not mitigate, are incurred in the transportation and processing of food.
70   More significant, however, is the fundamental fallacy that lies at the heart of the expansion of organic farming. Though some people have forgotten, conventional farming became the norm in the 1960s precisely
75   because it offered extraordinary yields without a considerable increase in cultivated land. The production of grains, for example, has tripled around the world, with an increase of only ten percent in the amount of land under cultivation.
80   When compared with conventional farming, the crop yields of organic farming are several times less. Thus, much more land is required for organic farming to produce the same amount of food. This fact means that, in order
85   to keep the current food crop stable, the amount of land utilized for organic farming would have to increase by several times its current level. In short, organic farming and its "environmental friendliness" would require the
90   voluminous destruction of natural habitats around the world. Forests and swamps would vanish, as would rainforests and wetlands, all in the name of environmental responsibility.

11. The authors of Passage 1 and Passage 2 would most likely disagree about

(A) the validity of the claims made by organic farmers
(B) the extent of the threat presented by artificial pesticides and fertilizers
(C) the amount of energy consumption required to sustain organic farming
(D) the level of acceptance of organic produce among consumers
(E) the necessity for transportation of organic foods from farms to markets

12. The authors of Passage 1 and Passage 2 would most likely agree that organic farming

(A) financially benefits all of its practitioners
(B) saves the energy normally expended in the conveyance of synthetic fertilizers
(C) is gradually replacing farming practices established in the 1960s
(D) can sustain current worldwide crop yields
(E) helps to prevent all soil and water pollution

13. Which of the following facts would most undermine the argument made in lines 3-10?

(A) The certification standards for the organic label vary from country to country
(B) Consumers pay an increased price for food that is certified organic.
(C) The organic farming industry spends millions of dollars in advertising.
(D) Organic farmers receive only a small percentage from each sale of organic food.
(E) A small minority of customers account for all the sales of organic foods.

14. In lines 16-22, the author primarily cites the danger of

(A) natural pesticides and fertilizers
(B) water and soil pollution
(C) soil erosion
(D) excessive energy consumption
(E) drinking water

15. In line 35, the word "redeems" most nearly means

(A) restores
(B) fulfills
(C) recovers
(D) saves
(E) ransoms

16. Lines 44-47 primarily serve to

(A) undermine a contradictory argument
(B) pose a theoretical conclusion about those who practice organic farming
(C) reassess a previously stated opinion about the feasibility of organic farming
(D) make a bold prediction
(E) satirize opponents of organic farming

17. In lines 51-54, the author of Passage 2 primarily suggests that

(A) the greatest advocates of organic foods are biased due to their financial interest
(B) organic farmers are responsible for the inflated costs of organic food
(C) consumers of organic foods remain unable to enumerate the benefits of organic farming
(D) the arguments of organic food advocates are insincere
(E) organic food products are more seriously flawed than non-organic products

18. Lines 66-69 primarily state that
(A) the transport costs of organic foods are expensive
(B) the shipping of farm food should be halted
(C) organic farming expends much energy in transport
(D) organic foods' benefits are negated by shipping
(E) organic farmers encourage the growth of weeds

19. In line 75, the word "yields" most nearly means

(A) resignations
(B) submissions
(C) outputs
(D) earnings
(E) concessions

20. The author of passage 2 most likely places the phrase "environmental friendliness" (line 89) in quotation marks in order to

(A) highlight the incongruity between the goal and the reality of the expansion of organic farming
(B) point out the deceitfulness of the arguments made by organic farmers
(C) parody the ignorance of those consumers who regularly purchase organic foods
(D) accentuate the poor nutrition of organic crops in comparison to that of conventional crops
(E) dispel the pervasive misconception that organic farming saves the rain forest

21. If asked to select the most serious omission in Passage 2, the author of Passage 1 would most likely choose

(A) the economic impact of organic farming
(B) the health benefits of organic foods
(C) the energy costs of food transport and processing
(D) the global success of organic food movements
(E) the pollution caused by conventional farming

22. The author of Passage 2 would most likely label the argument made in lines 32-40 as

(A) disingenuous
(B) incomplete
(C) reproachful
(D) confounded
(E) obsequious

23. In line 90, the word "voluminous" most nearly means

(A) winding
(B) ample
(C) bulky
(D) full
(E) vast

24. In line 92-93, the phrase "all in the name of environmental responsibility" is primarily an example of

(A) allusion
(B) irony
(C) simile
(D) personification
(E) alliteration

END SECTION

Practice Test 2
Answer Key and Explanations

Section1

1. B
2. C
3. D
4. D
5. A
6. D
7. C
8. D
9. A
10. B
11. E
12. D
13. C
14. D
15. B
16. E
17. B
18. A
19. D
20. A
21. C
22. C
23. A
24. D

Section 2

1. C
2. C
3. B
4. C
5. B
6. B
7. E
8. B
9. E
10. A

11. E
12. D
13. C
14. B
15. C
16. B
17. E
18. C
19. E

Section 3

1. C
2. C
3. C
4. E
5. B
6. C
7. E
8. C
9. B
10. D
11. C
12. B
13. E
14. B
15. D
16. D
17. A
18. C
19. C
20. A
21. E
22. B
23. E
24. B

Finding Your Score

Raw score: Total Number Right – [Total Number Wrong ÷ 4] = _____

Notes: 1) Omissions are not counted towards your raw score
         2) If the total number wrong ÷ 4 ends in .5 or .75, it is rounded up

\multicolumn{4}{c}{**Critical Reading Scoring Table**}			
Raw Score	**Scaled Score**	**Raw Score**	**Scaled Score**
67	800	32	540
66	800	31	530
65	800	30	520
64	800	29	520
63	780	28	510
62	770	27	500
61	760	26	500
60	740	25	490
59	730	24	480
58	720	23	470
57	710	22	460
56	700	21	460
55	690	20	450
54	680	19	440
53	670	18	430
52	660	17	430
51	660	16	420
50	650	15	420
49	640	14	400
48	630	13	390
47	630	12	380
46	620	11	370
45	610	10	370
44	610	9	360
43	600	8	350
42	590	7	340
41	590	6	330
40	580	5	320
39	580	4	310
38	570	3	300
37	560	2	280
36	560	1	260
35	550	0	240
34	550	-1	220
33	540	-2	200

Strength and Weakness Review

Go back to the test and circle the questions that you answered incorrectly. This review will allow you to see what answer explanations to study more closely for problem-solving techniques. It will also allow you to see what question types and passage types you need to review more carefully.

	Section 1	Section 2	Section 3
Passage Types			
Aesthetics / Arts			
Biography			
Fiction			
History	13-19		7-10
Hard Sciences	9-12	6-19	11-24
Social Sciences	20-24		
Question Types			
Assumption			
Attitude / Tone	19, 24	12, 18	
Inference	9, 14, 15, 16, 21, 22	9, 14, 16, 17, 19	13, 17, 21, 22
Literal Comprehension	10, 13, 18	11, 13, 15	9, 11, 12, 14, 18
Main Idea			7
Primary Purpose	20		8
Structure	12	6, 7	16, 20, 24
Word-in-Context	11, 17, 23	8, 10	10, 15, 19, 23

Section 1

1. B (indomitable: *strong*)

(A) indulgent: *obedient*
(C) unceasing: *long-lived*
(D) eclectic: *different / odd*
(E) stalwart: *brave*

2. C (timidity...timorous)
    afraid...afraid

(A) homogeneity...incredulous
    same...questioning
(B) rancor...zealous
    hate...passionate
(D) temerity...insipid
    brave...stupid
(E) amalgamation...apprehensive
    different...afraid

3. D (robust: *strong*)

(A) conventional: *same*
(B) vapid: *stupid*
(C) acquiescent: *obedient*
(E) voluminous: *a lot*

4. D (acceding: *obedient*)

(A) inexorable: *strong*
(B) pertinent: *relevant*
(C) vapid: *stupid*
(E) invincible: *strong*

5. A (detrimental: *harmful*)

(B) nonchalant: i*ndifferent*
(C) vapid: *stupid*
(D) insuperable: *strong*
(E) acquiescent: *obedient*

6. D (trite: *clichéd*)

(A) dubious: *questioning*
(B) meticulous: *careful*
(C) benevolent: *generous*
(E) affluent: *rich*

7. C (covertly...clandestine)
    secretive...secretive

(A) cogently...immaterial
    relevant...irrelevant
(B) stealthily...timorous
    secretive...afraid
(D) shrewdly...cajoling
    smart...to flatter
(E) blatantly...defamatory
    obvious...to insult

8. D (discrepant...salient)
    different...relevant

(A) stalwart...inscrutable
    brave...secretive
(B) indistinguishable...motley
    same...different
(C) derisive...obtuse
    to insult...stupid
(E) dubious...indomitable
    questioning...brave

9. A (Scope: *Passage 1 and Passage 2*)
In lines 19-21, the author of passage 1 states that individuals do experience emotions subjectively. The main idea of Passage 2 is that subjectivity is an essential component of emotions.

10. B (Scope: *Passage 1 and Passage 2*)
Author 1 repeatedly argues that hormones are the cause of emotions, and flatly states it in lines 1-2. Author 2, on the other hand, argues that individuals are the cause of emotions.

11. E (Scope: *Line 33*)
The context sentence states that "correlations" must be done, or "performed", with individuals.

12. D (Scope: *Passage 1 and Passage 2*)
The author of Passage 2 uses personal voice ("I") in lines 42-43.

13. C (Scope: *Lines 14-16*)
This choice contains the key ideas found in the lines: "language", "revolution", and "equal".

14. D (Scope: *Lines 17-19*)
Here is the distinction between the outlook of "today" (18) and the outlook of the past which sees de Gouges statements as "radical" (unconventional) .

15. B (Scope: *Lines 28-30*)
Her "disillusionment" (29) implies that her ideas were not accepted, as does the "contempt" (28) shown to her by the revolutionaries.

16. E (Scope: *Line 32*)
The quote previews the distinctly non-legal opinion as to the cause of her death: "She wanted to be a man." (33-34)

17. B (Scope: *Line 41*)
The sentence states that women must "uplift" their faculties, a meaning that comes closest to "grow" or "nurture".

18. A (Scope: *Lines 49-53*)
Only this choice contains the key people mentioned in the lines: Wollstonecraft and men.

19. D (Scope: *Whole Passage*)
Since Wollstonecraft crafts her appeal to men, it is likely that de Gouge, who appealed to women, would be skeptical.

20. A (Scope: *Whole Passage*)
The choice contains the central idea of "history", as well as that of the approaches: "traditionalists" (2nd paragraph) and "factualists" (3rd paragraph)

21. C (Scope: *Line 3*)
Only choice (C) captures the contrast between a single phrase ("born in", line 5) and the entire book ("600 pages", line 3).

22. C (Scope: *Lines 20-23*)
"The rise to success from humble beginnings" (line 21) is exemplified best by choice (C).

23. A (Scope: *Line 24*)
In the passage, the word "implicitly" is contrasted with the word "explicitly" or obviously. "Tacitly" is the best fit for the context.

24. D (Scope: *Lines 6 & 10*)
According to the passage, the traditionalists view historical inaccuracies as part of a larger goal. Since the people view the change as "trivial" (7), or unimportant, the traditionalists would be unlikely to agree with them, or be cynical of their perspective.

Section 2

1. C (a tangential...trenchant)
  irrelevant...relevant

(A) an apt...pusillanimous
  relevant...afraid
(B) an aberrant...indomitable
  odd...brave
(D) a homogeneous...quizzical
  same...confused
(E) an ingenious...acclaimed
  smart...to praise

2. C (covertly…clandestine)
secretive…secretive

(A) cogently…immaterial
relevant…irrelevant
(B) stealthily…timorous
secretive…afraid
(D) shrewdly…cajoling
smart…to flatter
(E) blatantly…defamatory
obvious…to insult

3. B (despondent: *depressed*)

(A) meticulous: *careful*
(C) vigorous: *strong*
(D) dubious: *questioning*
(E) reclusive: *shy*

4. C (extraneous: *irrelevant*)

(A) precocious: *mature*
(B) languid: *lazy / indifferent*
(D) succinct: *short*
(E) concurring: *agree*

5. B (disparity: *different*)

(A) penury: *poor*
(C) amelioration: *make better*
(D) brevity: *short*
(E) languidness: *lazy / indifferent*

6. B (Scope: *1ˢᵗ Paragraph*)

The first paragraph is a short story ("an anecdote") that the author uses in order to introduce ("to broach") the topic of metacognition.

7. E (Scope: *Lines 16-18*)

The referenced quote is extended upon in the following sentence (lines 19-22), in which the term "metacognition" is used to describe the author's action as a child.

8. B (Scope: *Line 35*)

In context, the word "bare" is used to describe a low ability to deal with stress. The idea of "a little" is best captured by "scanty".

9. E (Scope: *2ⁿᵈ Paragraph*)

As defined in the passage, metacognition is the ability to "think about thinking" (lines 21-22). Only choice (E) illustrates this idea.

10. A (Scope: *Line 47*)

In context, the author states the idea that the differences between those with high levels of self-control and those with low levels are very large, or noticeable. "Pronounced" fits this context the best.

11. E (Scope: *Lines 31-34*)

Only choice (E) captures the key ideas found in the lines: four-year-olds, self-control, and prediction ("prognostication").

12. D (Scope: *Whole Passage*)

In the passage, the author simply relates facts in a tone that neither praises nor condemns the ideas. This neutral tone is best exemplified by the phrase "measured objectivity."

13. C (Scope: *Lines 44-46*)

The referenced lines give a potential explanation ("the latter's ability to study or complete homework…") for the facts in lines 38-41.

14. B (Scope: *Lines 50-55*)

With the phrase "…it may not matter much", the author turns her attention from genes ("one of the factors") to the ability to teach gratification delay ("known factors").

15. C (Scope: *Lines 61-65*)

Only choice (C) contains all of the key ideas within the lines: young children, skills, and gratification delay.

16. B (Scope: *Lines 31-34*)

The author bases the lines on the results of tests that measure levels of self-control. Since choice (B) would directly invalidate the results of these tests, it would most effectively undermine the author's statement.

17. E (Scope: *Lines 57-61*)

In order for the author's mother to "pass on," or teach, metacognition, she herself would have to have learned the skill.

18. C (Scope: *Whole Passage*)

In lines 71-74 the author says that schools should be "encouraged" (hence, "optimistic"), but with the "caveat" ("cautious") that the schools must be careful to develop the skill into a habit among their students.

19. E (Scope: *Lines 46-49*)

Only choice (E) contains all of the key ideas of the lines: low levels of self-control and addictions.

Section 3

1. C (pithy...rambling)
   concise...irrelevant

(A) enigmatic...ephemeral
   secret...short-lived
(B) disinterested...tangential
   indifferent...irrelevant
(D) cursory...steadfast
   short-lived...same
(E) abiding...fatuous
   long-lived...stupid

2. C (attributed: *credit*)

(A) allayed: *make better*
(B) precluded: *stop*
(D) concurred: *agree*
(E) inundated: *flooded*

3. C (dauntless...audacious)
   brave...brave

(A) indubitable...jeering
   true...mocking
(B) applicable...stealthy
   relevant...secretive
(D) inane...pervasive
   stupid...widespread
(E) jaded...listless
   indifferent...indifferent

4. E (deviated...homogeneity)
   different...same

(A) touted...discrepancy
   to praise...different
(B) denigrated...uniformity
   to insult...same
(C) contradicted...eclecticism
   to argue against...odd
(D) digressed...nonchalance
   irrelevant...indifferent

5. B (augment: *make large*)

(A) vacillate: *unsure*
(C) preclude: *stop*
(D) concur: *agree*
(E) allay: *make better*

6. C (succinct: *short*)

(A) astute: *smart*
(B) precocious: *mature*
(D) scanty: *a little*
(E) extraneous: *irrelevant*

7. E (Scope: *Passages 1 and 2*)
The main ideas are "Lindbergh" and "history" (line 1; line 20). Only choice (E) contains both of these ideas.

8. C (Scope: *Passage 2*)
Since purpose questions encompass the entire passage, the answer must again include the ideas of "Lindbergh" and "history". Only choice (C) correctly does so.

9. B (Scope: *Line 9 and Passage 2*)
The key phrase is "later eclipsed by an inexcusable act", which the author summarizes in lines 27-31.

10. D (Scope: *Line 20*)
Within the context sentence, the word "moment" is accentuating the prominence and standing of the president, FDR. Only the word "importance" fits this intention.

11. C (Scope: *Passage 1 and Passage 2*)
In lines 32-33, the author of passage 1 states that organic farming uses *less* energy. In lines 56-57,the author of Passage 2 asserts that organic farming actually consumes *more* energy.

12. B (Scope: *Passage 1 and Passage 2*)
The assertion that the energy of transport costs is saved in organic farming is stated in lines 37-38(Passage 1) and in lines 57-60 (Passage 2).

13. E (Scope: *Lines 3-10*)
The key ideas in these lines are "consumers" and "organic food purchases". The best argument against the stated idea is to show that the same small group of people buys all organic food, thereby destroying the idea of widespread support.

14. B (Scope: *Lines 16-22*)
Soil pollution is addressed in line 17, and the idea of water pollution is addressed in lines19-22.

15. D (Scope: *Line 35*)
In context, the word "redeems" must have a definition similar to that of "saved" (line 37).

16. D (Scope: *Lines 44-47*)
In these lines, the author of Passage 1 shifts the focus from present practices to the future. Only the idea of a "prediction" fits the context of the future.

17. A (Scope: *Lines 51-54*)
The focus of these lines is the largest "proponents" (51) of organic farming. Only choice (A) addresses this group.

18. C (Scope: *Lines 66-69*)
The referenced "costs" are the energy costs of organic farming expended in the process of transporting its goods.

19. C (Scope: *Line 75*)
In context "yields" is used in the context of farming and "production" (line 77). Only "output" fits this context.

20. A (Scope: *Line 89*)
In these lines, the author continues to delineate what she calls a "fundamental fallacy" (line 71). This idea of falsehood therefore applies to "environmental friendliness" of organic farming, which the author disputes in lines 88-93.

21. E (Scope: *Passage 1 and Passage 2*)
The author of passage 1 includes the idea of pollution in lines 11-31. Since the author includes this idea, he would most likely view its absence in Passage 2 as the most serious.

22. B (Scope: *Lines 32-40, Passage 2*)
Since the author of Passage 2 refutes the ideas in lines 32-40 by presenting further information, she would most likely view the argument in Passage 1 as incomplete.

23. E (Scope: *Line 90*)

The word "voluminous" continues the idea begun by the phrase "increase by several times" (line 87). Only "vast" captures this idea of largeness.

24. B (Scope: *Lines 92-93*)

The author uses irony to highlight the difference between the aim of environmental protection and the actual result of environmental destruction.

SAT CRITICAL READING PRACTICE TEST 3

Time: 25 Minutes
24 Questions

Directions: Choose the answer that is grammatically correct, concise, and unambiguous.

1. Despite all her efforts to ----- the stampede, the cattle charged past her and galloped free into the sunset.

(A) disdain   (B) ameliorate   (C) exonerate
     (D) impede   (E) retract

2. Instead of defending her client with information ----- the case, the lawyer attempted to distract the jury with immaterial, ----- arguments.

(A) timorous of...antagonistic
(B) incredulous of...malignant
(C) pertinent...digressive
(D) adulatory of...lackadaisical
(E) discordant to...foolhardy

3. The test day was a ----- event; the students marked it with solemnity and a tinge of sadness.

(A) hackneyed   (B) scanty   (C) somber
     (D) benevolent   (E) superfluous

4. The models were judged on a single -----; their only responsibility was to mimic clothes hangers as expertly as possible.

(A) aberration   (B) criterion (C) attribution
     (D) disparity   (E) monotony

5. Her neighbors described the old woman as ----- due to the fact that she obsessively collected plastic bats and bandaged rats.

(A) sympathetic   (B) uniform   (C) spurious
     (D) eccentric   (E) detrimental

6. The sponge monkey is an ----- creature; it has been seen in the wild only a handful of times.

(A) apathetic   (B) eclectic   (C) inclusive
     (D) elusive   (E) assiduous

7. Astronomy has shown that the formation of stars is by no means ----- event, but rather ----- phenomenon that occurs on a consistent basis.

(A) an incontrovertible...a disingenuous
(B) a vacuous...a quixotic
(C) a spiteful...an undaunted
(D) a specious...an incidental
(E) an anomalous...a constant

8. For all of her ----- in abstract math, and she is a recognized sage in the field, Sonja has made ---- career choices that have left her destitute,

(A) discursiveness...pervasive
(B) veracity...prosperous
(C) eclecticism...uniform
(D) antagonism...intrepid
(E) acumen...imbecilic

Questions 9-16 are based on the following passage.

The English poet, A.E. Housman, once struggled to describe the color of a garden while composing a poem. After he had tried and discarded "green," "green-blue,"
5   "greenish," "bluish" and "dark bluish", he asked a friend for help. When the friend confidently identified the garden as dark blue, Housman shook his head in resignation and said, "It's impossible. We need a Chinese
10 speaker."

Housman's response points to the belief in a cultural and linguistic component of color perception. Psychologists who would sympathize with this remark contend that the
15 spectrum can be divided anyplace along its length, based on an individual's native language. This view holds that an object described by one person as blue may be described by a person with a different mother
20 tongue as green. For instance, speakers of Welsh use one word for green. However, their word for "grass" literally translates as "blue straw". For the Welsh speaker, therefore, the division between blue and green is pliable,
25 with blue possessing the capacity to incorporate all shades of green.

Other psychologists dismiss the effects of environment and instead advocate a genetic explanation for the human perception of hues.
30 According to this view, color discrimination is innate. That is, the brain is preconditioned to classify the six primary colors, and each person does so similarly regardless of their native tongue. All languages therefore allocate words
35 around the same six hues. In at least one study, in which 110 different languages were compared, this theory held true across more than 330 shades of color.

It seems that both theories may be correct,
40 that there exists both an intrinsic color distinction and one that is mediated through language. Yet the precise interaction between congenital and linguistic effects remains to be discovered, a shortcoming in understanding
45 that is starkly highlighted by the Amazonian tribe, the Pirahã. Members of this tribe seem to possess no fixed words for colors. Instead, the Pirahã employ shifting descriptive phrases to describe color. So, if they see a brown shirt,

50 they might say, "This looks like tree bark", or "This looks like river mud".

If a full understanding of the process of color perception is to be achieved, psychologists must study cases such as the
55 Pirahã to a much fuller extent. Otherwise, we will be left shaking our collective head in frustration, like Housman, at the imperfection of perception.

9. Lines 1-10 primarily serve the role of

(A) Invoking a rebuttal
(B) Proffering a thesis
(C) Recounting a personal anecdote
(D) Revealing an inherent contradiction
(E) Introducing a topic

10. Which of the following situations most closely resembles that described in lines 17-20?

(A) A native Russian speaker and a native Japanese speaker cannot communicate
(B) A native English speaker and a native Zulu speaker disagree about a painter's use of color
(C) A native Urdu speaker and a native Spanish speaker have the same favorite color
(D) A native Chinese speaker and a native Arabic speaker cannot agree on the hue of a sunset
(E) A native German speaker and a native Portuguese speaker cannot decide on the best color for a new car that they are buying

11. In line 30, "discrimination" most nearly means

(A) notice
(B) discernment
(C) prejudice
(D) judgment
(E) opinion

12. In lines 31-34, the assumption is made that

(A) only six principal colors exist within the entire spectrum of colors
(B) Welsh speakers perceive the color of grass based upon innate information
(C) the brain is not primarily responsible for the discrimination of color
(D) native languages condition the brain and its differentiation of color
(E) deviation among languages is responsible for differing perceptions of color

13. The "other psychologists" (line 27) would most likely blame Housman's problem (paragraph 1) on

(A) his friend's incompetence with language
(B) his genetic inability to perceive the correct color
(C) his limitations as a native English speaker
(D) his unfamiliarity with the color spectrum
(E) his lack of access to a native Chinese speaker

14. In lines 39-42, the author offers

(A) an example that supports previous opinions
(B) a reevaluation of unexpected circumstances
(C) a refutation of commonly-held beliefs
(D) a narration of distinctive events
(E) a reconciliation of opposing theories

15. In line 47, the word "fixed" most nearly means

(A) resolute
(B) flat
(C) stationary
(D) definite
(E) immobile

16. The primary purpose of the passage is to

(A) invalidate the genetic component of color differentiation
(B) corroborate the necessity of color in poetry
(C) point out the consequences of color perception among people around the world
(D) vindicate the view that language determines an individual's discernment of color
(E) clarify the current state of knowledge of color perception among humans

Questions 17-24 are based on the following passage.

The rise of the novel in the 18th century produced an outcry that is difficult to imagine today. Novel-reading was denounced for creating immodest behavior, self-absorption,
5 and a general decline in morality. One critic even went so far as to compare novels to the Black Death, which had killed approximately half the population of Europe in the 1340s. Given this context, it is ironic that the death of
10 the novel itself has provoked such an outraged cacophony in recent times.

The most popular alarmists generally point towards the same culprit: the digitization of novels. As more and more novels are scanned
15 and made available in digital form, their theory holds, books as objects will soon disappear and be replaced by computers. Since the book form and novels are inextricably bound, the novel will also die. Supporters of this theory often
20 point to the example of the album, which has all but vanished in favor of collections of digitized songs.

It is a mistake to equate the novel with the album, however, insofar as novels are not as
25 easily transferable as music. One can easily upload an old song into a portable player, whereas one cannot upload one's old novels into any similar device. In fact, a better analogy may be drawn between the novel and
30 the CD. Not only has free access to digital songs not meant the demise of the CD, it has actually spurred CD sales by whetting people's appetite for the music. As the digitization of novels progresses, it is likely that online
35 readers will use digital copies in order to preview the work. If satisfied, they will then purchase the novel from a bookstore or borrow the book from a library.

Yet, there is a more abstract and more
40 powerful argument for the continuing existence of novels: human need. The computer screen is a cold companion, with no feeling and no interaction. A book, on the other hand, has weight and character. People incorporate books
45 into their lives, bringing them into their bathtubs, their beds, and out to beaches for unhurried reading and reflection. In short, an ineffable relationship takes place between a paper novel and its reader.

50 For books are not chiefly objects, or even a neutral medium for the conveyance of ideas. Instead, they are markers of people's thoughts and feelings. As one novelist has expressed it, "Books do not sit quietly on shelves. They live
55 incessantly in the hearts and minds. For this reason must we discuss them in the present tense…Books are souvenirs of the ways we have felt and the way we have lived."

17. What is the main subject of the passage?

(A) the history of the novel as a literary genre
(B) the resemblance between the CD and the book as a medium of art
(C) the continued existence of novels as books
(D) the outrages caused by novels throughout history
(E) the ongoing digitization of novels

18. In line 4, the word "immodest" most nearly means

(A) extravagant
(B) indecent
(C) conceited
(D) bold
(E) extraordinary

19. Lines 14-17 primarily indicate that

(A) alarmists fear the innate capabilities of computers
(B) digitalization ensures the existence of books
(C) the demise of the novel is a lamentable event
(D) the novel and the album are equivalent mediums
(E) the digitalization of books is progressing rapidly

20. What would be the most likely attitude of the "critic" (line 5) to the scenario described in lines 17-19?

(A) uneasy incredulity
(B) total apathy
(C) scornful derision
(D) satisfied approval
(E) wild befuddlement

21. The author's argument in the 3rd paragraph rests primarily on the assumption that

(A) CDs are more accepted than are novels
(B) the digitalization of novels remains inferior to that of music
(C) new novels are radically different than old novels
(D) people will behave towards digitalized novels as they have towards digitalized music
(E) libraries and bookstores provide the same service for readers of novels

22. The primary distinction made in lines 41-47 is one between

(A) disconnection and engagement
(B) technology and tradition
(C) novels and readers
(D) rationality and emotion
(E) existence and death

23. In line 51, the word "conveyance" most nearly means

(A) transportation
(B) articulation
(C) manifestation
(D) transmittance
(E) granting

24. In the final two paragraphs, the structure can best be described as

(A) a harsh rebuke followed by a humorous anecdote
(B) an ironic parody followed by a bold vindication
(C) a great abstraction followed by a final conclusion
(D) a practical account followed by a valid criticism
(E) a new assertion followed by a supporting citation

END SECTION

Time: 25 Minutes
24 Questions

Directions: Choose the answer that is grammatically correct, concise, and unambiguous.

---

1. As cell phones have become -----, gaining a conventional place in society, phone booths have become ---- and arcane relics of the past.

(A) commonplace…esoteric
(B) anomalous…eccentric
(C) cerebral…discordant
(D) resolute…listless
(E) incredulous…trenchant

2. While his ----- and genius for building hotels was legendary, his unwavering, ----- desire to build one inside a volcano was widely questioned.

(A) beneficence…covetous
(B) delineation…fraudulent
(C) vacuity…germane
(D) acumen…resolute
(E) liberality…conventional

3. Mr. Ahn ----- for avocadoes as a lobbyist, promoting increased consumption of the fruit.

(A) empathizes   (B) advocates   (C) belies
    (D) discloses   (E) amasses

4. The Global Anteater Society is an ----- organization which welcomes members of all ages, races, and nationalities.

(A) antagonistic   (B) ephemeral   (C) inclusive
    (D) innate   (E) eclectic

5. Inner-city schools are moving from more diverse student populations to more ----- ones.

(A) reticent   (B) homogeneous   (C) ephemeral
    (D) pervasive   (E) specious

Questions 6-9 are based on the following passages.

Passage 1

Critics may yet be justified in their accusations of alarmism in the media. However, with the rise of the Internet, their targeting of the media is misplaced. It is not
5　media outlets but rather the public that increasingly determines the popularity and longevity of news stories through interactive polls and ratings systems. In these forums, the public's general preference for fear over
10　comfort is clear. As one prominent psychologist writes, "People simply pay more attention, and respond more vigorously, to the negative." So, if anxiety is a permanent part of the media, we have only ourselves to fault.

Passage 2

15　　Daily, the media assaults the public with dire warnings and prognostications. News reports seem to suggest that we all are just waiting victims of SARS or deadly shark attacks. Never mind that, statistically,
20　bathrooms represent a greater threat to humans than do either of these perceived threats. Taken at face value, the kind of hyperbole in which the media engages may seem laughably innocuous. Yet this exaggeration harms us all,
25　not only by limiting the spectrum of available information, but also by obscuring the true dangers to public safety.

6. The primary purpose of Passage 1 is to

(A) denounce the media's use of the Internet and other interactive tools
(B) defend the public's symbiotic relationship with the media
(C) delineate the process through which the media creates alarm
(D) advocate the necessity for fear among the public
(E) account for the pervasive presence of fear within the media

7. In Passage 2, the attitude of the author towards the media can best be described as one of

(A) mild perplexity
(B) awed appreciation
(C) scornful indignation
(D) general indifference
(E) marked cynicism

8. The authors of Passage 1 and Passage 2 would most likely agree that

(A) the media should bear criticism for its actions
(B) the public must be shielded from the most grave threats to its safety
(C) fear is a substantial presence in the media
(D) the public's reaction to the media is in line with its reactions to other facets of life
(E) the media produces fear for its own benefit

9. Unlike the author of Passage 2, the author of Passage 1

(A) proposes a solution
(B) recounts a personal experience
(C) cites an authority
(D) offers statistical support
(E) refutes a common myth

Questions 10-16 are based on the following passage.

It's a natural progression. Traditional terrestrial mines are rapidly becoming depleted. The rate of discoveries of new land deposits continues to dwindle. At the same
5　time, huge middle classes are emerging across the globe, particularly in India and China. This upward mobility has created unprecedented global demand for copper, iron, and zinc. The time is ripe for the mining of the ocean.
10　Minerals exist in large quantities on the ocean floor, particularly around extinct smokers. When these geological formations are active, heated water shoots through the Earth's crust and picks up minerals. As the deposits
15　cool, they form mineral-rich rock formations. These tall chimneys represent not only a great source of minerals but a great opportunity.

Underwater mining can provide the benefits of terrestrial mining without its ills.
20　No longer would unlucky remote societies suffer in order to fulfill the desires of other societies. No longer would indigenous societies be displaced from their homelands in order to accommodate the exploitation of new mineral
25　finds. While this benefit in no way addresses the multitude of previous injustices, it does promise to ensure that no further injustices are perpetrated in the name of mining.

Furthermore, the environmental
30　devastation often caused by terrestrial mining would be avoided. No land would be scarred by open pits and no mountains leveled. A pervasive danger would no longer be posed by cyanide, which terrestrial mines utilize in order
35　to extract minerals from rock.

Near the smokers of the oceans, on the other hand, the effects of mining will be minimal. According to recent marine studies, few animal species exist in these harsh
40　conditions, far from the light of the sun. Those animals that do exist are hardy and conditioned to turmoil, which erupts constantly with the changing conditions precipitated by the volcanic activity of the Earth's crust.

10. The structure of lines 1-9 can best be characterized as

(A) a refutation followed by a series of scientific realities
(B) a justification followed by a sociological survey
(C) a specious statement followed by a correction
(D) a salient issue followed by a long digression
(E) an assertion followed by substantiating details

11. Lines 6-8 primarily imply that

(A) middle classes are responsible for the initiation of underwater mining
(B) India and China are at the forefront of underwater mining technology
(C) the mining industry has helped in the emergence of a vast middle class
(D) terrestrial mines can no longer supply certain metals
(E) the growth of middle classes is accompanied by an increased demand for certain resources

12. Lines 10-15 primarily serve to

(A) satirize opponents of underwater mining
(B) account for the presence of minerals in the ocean
(C) demystify the life cycle of geological smokers
(D) validate the existence of minerals in the ocean
(E) underscore the benefits of underwater mining

13. In line 25, the word "addresses" most nearly means

(A) approaches
(B) directs
(C) focuses
(D) deals with
(E) transmits

14. Lines 22-25 primarily imply that

(A) indigenous societies often take advantage of
    new mineral finds
(B) mineral discoveries are commonplace in
    homelands
(C) underwater mining can redress previous
    instances of injustices
(D) terrestrial mining sometimes involves the
    displacement of indigenous societies
(E) indigenous societies are inherently unlucky

15. Which of the following facts would best
undermine the argument made in lines 38-40?

(A) The animals that exist near ocean smokers are
    members of endangered species.
(B) Volcanic activity on the ocean floor is only
    periodic and limited in scope.
(C) The underwater mining industry commissioned
    the referenced scientific studies.
(D) Some of the species on the ocean floor are
    stronger than others.
(E) The Earth's crust is unpredictable and prone to
    constant shifts.

16. The author most likely uses the phrase "far from
the light of the sun" (line 40) in order to

(A) vindicate the remoteness of marine animals
(B) point out the challenges faced in the extraction
    of underwater minerals
(C) punctuate the severity of the environment near
    the ocean floor
(D) refute the necessity of the sun for existence
(E) denigrate the terrestrial mining industry for the
    environmental damage it causes

Questions 17-24 are based on the following passages.

It was great to be home again. If the town appeared slightly different than when I had left, well it was most certainly due to my now sophisticated eyes. If the townspeople no
5 longer responded to my greetings with the same vigor, then it was undoubtedly a sign of noble restraint. Some of the most benevolent people even went so far as to cross the street at the first sign of my approach.
10 Though all made a concerted effort, perhaps no one exhibited such fine control from the very first as my neighbor, Mr. Crump. The moment that I pulled my bicycle into the driveway, arriving triumphantly to liberate my
15 grandmother from loneliness, he began to stand watch over me from his yard. "Living in the attic again, huh," he said, shaking his head.

I understood him immediately, of course. I would be wagging a deceitful tongue, however,
20 if I did not admit to some surprise. After all, while many in the city had made passing reference, rewarding me by quoting back such crafted words as "sun" and "red", they had each confined themselves to a specific poem.
25 None had possessed the subtlety to allude to three of my unpublished poems in a single strike.

From that point forward, Crump and I shared an intimate understanding. He would do
30 his best to nurture the solitude I required for artistic achievement, while I would work to immortalize the man in epic verse. This unspoken arrangement would remain steadfast.

When Crump stopped hanging up on me
35 and instead changed his phone number altogether, I realized that he was urging me to take a less superficial approach to his story. The poetry, he seemed to admonish, lie not in the details of a man but in his essence. When
40 he erected a solid fence between our properties, the message was writ ten-feet high: "divide the poem into two equal halves". When he then extended the fence to the sidewalk, forcing me to leave from and return to my house only from
45 the opposite direction, I knew instantly that the perspective of the poem was wrong.

Rereading the pages now, the benefits of shifting the poem from third-person to first-person cannot be underestimated. As "Crump:

50 An Epic Verse in Two Parts" nears its completion, after five arduous years, the excitement around town is palpable. Excited whispers, punctuated by exclamatory sounds, accompany my every trip outside the house. I
55 can only trust, after an anxious wait of more than nine months, that Mr. Crump will soon return from his vacation.

17. In line 6, the word "vigor" most nearly means

(A) enthusiasm
(B) effectiveness
(C) vitality
(D) strength
(E) validity

18. According to lines 7-9, the attitude of the townspeople towards the narrator can best be described as one of

(A) deep affection
(B) grand beneficence
(C) active disinclination
(D) genuine awe
(E) fawning adulation

19. In lines 25-27, the narrator primarily implies that

(A) city residents remained unaware of his poetry
(B) Crump struck down three of the his poems
(C) the three referenced poems were his favorite
(D) Crump intentionally referenced the three poems
(E) city residents were not as subtle as Crump

20. The passage primarily implies the arrangement between the narrator and Crump is "unspoken" (line 33) because

(A) the narrator is too modest to speak of it
(B) Crump prefers to be a silent patron of the arts
(C) the narrator and Crump only communicate silently
(D) Crump is oblivious to any such agreement
(E) the narrator advocates communication through verse

21. Lines 34-46 primarily constitute a series of

(A) rebukes towards a former mentor
(B) unrelated acts executed by individuals
(C) responses to subtle motivations
(D) admonishments exchanged between neighbors
(E) reactions to misinterpreted deeds

22. According to the passage, the narrator shifts the voice of his epic verse from "third-person to first-person" (line 48-49) primarily in response to

(A) his deteriorating relationship with Crump
(B) the excited criticism of his poem by the
    townspeople
(C) Crump's refusal to communicate via telephone
(D) lessons that he learned from previous,
    unpublished poems
(E) Crump's elongation of the fence

23. According to the passage, Crump would most likely view his relationship with the narrator as one of

(A) reciprocated respect
(B) unmitigated irritation
(C) perpetual timorousness
(D) profound enmity
(E) mutual appreciation

24. Based on the passage, the "vacation" (line 57) can most likely be characterized as

(A) a brief sojourn
(B) an amusing journey
(C) an anxious trip
(D) a permanent relocation
(E) an exciting interlude

END SECTION

Time: 20 Minutes
19 Questions

Directions: Choose the answer that is grammatically correct, concise, and unambiguous.

1. Norbert's doctor assured him that his fungal condition was not a cause for ----- and that its treatment was cheap and would not ---- him.

(A) insolvency…deceive
(B) iconoclasm…rebuff
(C) extravagance…malign
(D) bewilderment…invalidate
(E) apprehension…pauperize

2. Shopping malls are ----- in the suburbs; each community has at least one.

(A) inclusive   (B) similar   (C) ephemeral
(D) spurious   (E) prevalent

3. The organization argued that its donation of 40,000 used pencils to the youth group was no ----- but rather a part of a pattern of ----.

(A) munificence…gluttony
(B) toady…uniformity
(C) aberration…magnanimity
(D) parody…perplexity
(E) chastisement…prodigality

4. He realized that although his justification was not entirely -----, neither was it completely ----- and incontrovertible.

(A) lavish…excursive
(B) covert…apt
(C) specious…indubitable
(D) eccentric…remunerative
(E) lukewarm…mendacious

5. Her decision to eat cheese was -----: she could have just as easily chosen bratwurst or pickles.

(A) eclectic   (B) arbitrary   (C) sage
(D) inherent   (E) homogeneous

6. The reintroduction of the three-toed sloth into the forest was designed to encourage its -----throughout the entire habitat.

(A) exclusiveness (B) antipathy (C) documentation
(D) reticence   (E) proliferation

Questions 7-8 are based on the following passage.

　　The term "alchemist" conjures up a host of shadowy images related to the transmutation of common metals into gold. While many alchemists honestly devoted their lives to this
5　endeavor, it is the charlatans who deceptively used alchemical promises that live on in the modern imagination. This situation is directly traceable to the pioneers of chemistry, who sought to distance their new science from the
10　"taint" of alchemy. Though these originators might be surprised to see the extent of their success today, they would certainly not miss the irony that modern chemistry's fundamental equipment and techniques were all developed
15　by alchemists.

7. Lines 3-7 primarily serve to

(A) illustrate the origins of modern chemistry
(B) reproach alchemy as a pseudo-science
(C) explicate the methods utilized by alchemists
(D) undermine the efforts of modern chemists
(E) differentiate between groups of alchemists

8. The main idea of the passage is

(A) alchemists' contribution to the science of chemistry
(B) chemistry's theft of the ideas and instruments of alchemy
(C) the processes of transmutation employed by alchemists
(D) the dichotomy between alchemy and chemistry
(E) modern chemists' disavowal of alchemists

Questions 9-10 are based on the following passage.

　　The word "robot" is utilized in hundreds of languages and cultures. Although the invention of the word is often attributed to the Czech playwright, Karel Capek, it was actually
5　his brother, Josef, who was the first to devise the term. It was Karel, however, who popularized the term by utilizing it in a play entitled *R.U.R.* (*Rossum's Universal Robots*) in order to denote a class of forced laborers. The
10　play was immensely successful in European countries and the United States. Interestingly, these countries still generally regard robots with the same attitudes embodied in the plot of Kapek's play. That is, the word "robot"
15　continues to hold the mixed emotions of skepticism, promise, and apprehension. In other countries that inherited the word more indirectly, however, the connotations attached to the word "robot" diverge widely from those
20　propagated by the play. In Japan, for example, robots provoke only positive feelings and the machines themselves have become an almost pedestrian feature of everyday life.

9. In line 5, the word "devise" most nearly means

(A) plan
(B) create
(C) transmit
(D) suppose
(E) scheme

10. In lines 11-14, the author primarily suggests that

(A) attitudes towards robots around the world have been fixed by the play, *R.U.R.*
(B) the Japanese are not familiar with *R.U.R.*
(C) robots are a crucial element of Kapek's play
(D) Kapek is to blame for the universality of robots
(E) *R.U.R.* continues to indirectly influence the opinion of robots in several countries

Questions 11-19 are based on the following passage.

In contrast to the movement of American artists to Europe in the 1920s, the emigration of American scientists received no contemporary notice. This situation is not surprising,
5 however, when one realizes that these latter emigrants were rarely considered to be either Americans or scientists, at least until they left their native country.

Percy Julian moved to Austria in 1929,
10 after spending nearly a decade attempting to obtain a doctorate in chemistry in the United States. After his graduation from DePauw College in 1921, Julian had been rejected by American doctorate programs, with the
15 dubious justification that their investment was not valuable for a man who would only find employment at a Black college. Harvard University had withdrawn his fellowship in 1923, citing concern that its white students
20 would resent his instruction. Only in 1929, with a move to the University of Vienna, was Julian able to recommence his graduate studies in chemistry.

Finally free to pursue his intellectual
25 ambitions, Julian thrived in the laboratories of Vienna. Yet, it is not discussions of academic emancipation that fill Julian's letters of the time. Rather they detail the manifestations of other liberties, both personal and intellectual.
30 For Vienna provided him, for the first time, with the opportunity to participate fully in intellectual gatherings and everyday society. His meticulous and exuberant accounts of even simple pastimes, such as watching movies and
35 attending the opera, provide a light that illuminates the dark shadows of his past experiences.

If Julian had traveled to Paris during this time, he may have met and shared a knowing
40 conversation with the biologist E.E. Just. Just had fled to France in 1929, hoping to escape the pervasive racism of his academic "colleagues", who urged him to pursue a more appropriate field. In Europe, he freely
45 continued his research on cells and cellular development. He championed an approach, based on his research on marine invertebrates, of cellular holism. That is, the idea that an organism cannot be explained by the sum of its
50 parts but rather only by the lively interactions between its many complex parts. Yet this dialogue between the two great scientists never occurred.

Julian returned to the United States in
55 1931, battling great odds to eventually synthesize testosterone and progesterone, helping to treat hormonal conditions, and to synthesize cortisone, a steroid with a wide range of medicinal uses. Just returned to the
60 United States in 1940, only under the threat of Nazis and the capture of Paris. When he died of cancer in 1941, he left behind a cornerstone approach for all biologists.

The scientific legacies of these two men
65 are undoubtedly secure. In an age of stagnant or declining doctoral achievement rates among Blacks, however, one must wonder what other legacies remain.

11. In lines 1-4, the author primarily implies that

(A) most American scientists moved to Europe in the 1920s
(B) emigration from America to Europe increased substantially in the 1920s
(C) most American artists emigrated to Europe in the 1920s
(D) American artistic movements enjoyed popularity in Europe in the 1920s
(E) American artists who emigrated to Europe in the 1920s garnered attention

12. In line 16, the word "valuable" most nearly means

(A) costly
(B) worthwhile
(C) precious
(D) inestimable
(E) important

13. According to the passage, "the dark shadows" (lines 36) most likely represent

(A) the threat of World War II
(B) the volatility of chemical mixtures
(C) the hardship of emigration
(D) the pressure of academic study
(E) the injustice of racial prejudice

14. In line 43, the author most likely places "colleagues" inside quotation marks in order to

(A) assert the strength of Just's academic friendships
(B) scoff at the collegial system of academic faculty
(C) stress the gap between Just and other academics
(D) debunk myths about the idea of collegiality
(E) show the disparity between America and France

15. Which of the following scenarios is most similar to the idea presented by the author in lines 48-51?

(A) A 500-piece jigsaw puzzle that, when put together, forms a picture of Mount Everest.
(B) Cans and bottles are sorted and placed in piles at a recycling center.
(C) Computer parts are gathered and assembled to make a new computer.
(D) Water is poured into an ice-cube tray and placed in the freezer to make ice cubes.
(E) A stamp collector gathers her stamps and places them in chronological order in an album.

16. The primary purpose of the passage is to

(A) refute common misconceptions about the emigration of Black scientists
(B) vindicate the scientific legacy of Percy Julian
(C) advocate the need for more Black scientists
(D) delineate the concept of cellular holism
(E) profile a pair of Black scientists

17. In line 59, the word "range" most nearly means

(A) pasture
(B) gamut
(C) class
(D) area
(E) habitat

18. In lines 65-68, the author's attitude can best be described as one of

(A) reverent awe
(B) perplexed irony
(C) marked dispassion
(D) measured cynicism
(E) passive apprehension

19. Lines 61-63 primarily state that

(A) Julian's achievements ultimately outweighed those of Just
(B) the Nazis were indirectly responsible for Just's death
(C) biologists later appreciated the efforts and achievements of Just
(D) cancer was always a fatal disease in 1941
(E) Just pioneered a method that helped future biologists

END SECTION

Practice Test 3
Answer Key and Explanations

Section1

1. D
2. C
3. C
4. B
5. D
6. D
7. E
8. E
9. E
10. D
11. B
12. A
13. B
14. E
15. D
16. E
17. C
18. B
19. E
20. D
21. D
22. A
23. D
24. E

Section 2

1. A
2. D
3. B
4. C
5. B
6. E
7. E
8. C
9. C

10. E
11. E
12. B
13. D
14. D
15. C
16. C
17. A
18. C
19. D
20. D
21. E
22. E
23. B
24. D

Section 3

1. E
2. E
3. C
4. C
5. B
6. E
7. E
8. A
9. B
10. E
11. E
12. B
13. E
14. C
15. C
16. E
17. B
18. D
19. E

.Finding Your Score

Raw score: Total Number Right – [Total Number Wrong ÷ 4] = _____

Notes: 1) Omissions are not counted towards your raw score
2) If the total number wrong ÷ 4 ends in .5 or .75, it is rounded up

Critical Reading Scoring Table

Raw Score	Scaled Score	Raw Score	Scaled Score
67	800	32	540
66	800	31	530
65	800	30	520
64	800	29	520
63	780	28	510
62	770	27	500
61	760	26	500
60	740	25	490
59	730	24	480
58	720	23	470
57	710	22	460
56	700	21	460
55	690	20	450
54	680	19	440
53	670	18	430
52	660	17	430
51	660	16	420
50	650	15	420
49	640	14	400
48	630	13	390
47	630	12	380
46	620	11	370
45	610	10	370
44	610	9	360
43	600	8	350
42	590	7	340
41	590	6	330
40	580	5	320
39	580	4	310
38	570	3	300
37	560	2	280
36	560	1	260
35	550	0	240
34	550	-1	220
33	540	-2	200

Strength and Weakness Review

Go back to the test and circle the questions that you answered incorrectly. This review will allow you to see what answer explanations to study more closely for problem-solving techniques. It will also allow you to see what question types and passage types you need to review more carefully.

	Section 1	Section 2	Section 3
Passage Types			
Aesthetics / Arts	17-24		9-10
Biography			11-19
Fiction		17-24	
History			7-8
Hard Sciences	9-16	10-16	
Social Sciences		6-9	
Question Types			
Assumption	12, 21		
Attitude / Tone	20	7, 18	18
Inference	10, 13	11, 14, 15, 16, 19, 20, 23, 24	10, 11, 13, 14, 15
Literal Comprehension	19, 22	8, 12, 21, 22	7, 19
Main Idea	17		8
Primary Purpose	16	6	16
Structure	9, 14, 24	9, 10	
Word-in-Context	11, 15, 18, 23	13, 17	9, 12, 17

Section 1

1. D (impede: *stop*)

(A) disdain: *hate*
(B) ameliorate: *make better*
(C) exonerate: *free from blame*
(E) retract: *take back*

2. C (pertinent...digressive)
    relevant...irrelevant

(A) timorous of…antagonistic
    afraid…hate
(B) incredulous of …malignant
    questioning…to insult
(D) adulatory of…lackadaisical
    flatter...indifferent
(E) discordant to…foolhardy
    dislike…stupid

3. C (somber: *depressed*)

(A) hackneyed: *clichéd*
(B) scanty: *a little*
(D) benevolent: generous
(E) superfluous: *unnecessary*

4. B (criterion: *standard*)

(A) aberration: *different*
(C) attribution: *credit*
(D) disparity: *different*
(E) monotony: *same*

5. D (eccentric: *different*)

(A) sympathetic: *feeling*
(B) uniform: *same*
(C) spurious: *false*
(E) detrimental: *harmful*

6. D (elusive: *hard to catch*)

(A) apathetic: *indifferent*
(B) eclectic: *different*
(C) inclusive: *including*
(E) assiduous: *hard-working*

7. E (an anomalous…a constant)
    different…same

(A) an incontrovertible…a disingenuous
    true…lying
(B) a vacuous…a quixotic
    stupid…odd
(C) a spiteful…an undaunted
    to insult...brave
(D) a specious …an incidental
    false…irrelevant

8. E (acumen...imbecilic)
    smart…stupid

(A) discursiveness…pervasive
    irrelevant…widespread
(B) veracity…prosperous
    true…rich
(C) eclecticism…uniform
    different...same
(D) antagonism…intrepid
    hate…brave

9. E (Scope: *Lines 1-10*)
The first paragraph is a story that focuses on color perception, thereby serving to introduce the topic that is addressed throughout the rest of the passage.

10. D (Scope: *Lines 17-20*)
The situation in the lines describes two people with different native languages looking at the same object and remaining unable to agree on the object's color. Only choice (D) adheres to this situation, with the object being the "sunset" and the two speakers of different languages unable to agree on its color.

11. B (Scope: *Line 30*)
The context sentence includes the idea of color perception. Only "discernment", or differentiation, fits this context.

12. A (Scope: *Lines 31-34*)
Within these lines, the idea is that genetics and not language determines color perception. More specifically, the brain groups colors around six main colors. This statement primarily assumes that only six primarily colors exist.

13. B (Scope: *Paragraph 1 and Paragraph 3*)
The "psychologists" (27) believe that genetics determines color perception. Therefore, they would most likely assign Housman's problem a genetic cause.

14. E (Scope: *Lines 39-42*)
These lines mention both theories of color perception, and states that they both may be right. Only choice (E) contains both theories and their possible reconciliation.

15. D (Scope: *Line 47*)
The context shows that the term "fixed" must have the opposite meaning of "shifting" (line 48) in terms of language and vocabulary. Only "definite" fits this context.

16. E (Scope: *Whole Passage*)
The author explains throughout the passage, so choices (A), (B), and (D) can be eliminated. Since the passage focuses on what is known about color perception, choice (E) is correct.

17. C (Scope: *Whole Passage*)
The passage is a discussion of the future existence of the novel in book form. Choice (B) wrongly focuses on the novel's history, while the other choices only cover small parts of the passage.

18. B (Scope: *Line 4*)
The context discusses a "decline in morality" (5) in connection with "immodest behavior". Thus the idea of "indecency" (4) best fits the context of the sentence.

19. E (Scope: *Line 14-17*)
The lines focus on digitalization and its threat to novels as books. Only choice (E) contains both of these ideas.

20. D (Scope: *Line 5 and Lines 17-19*)
Since the referenced "critic" decried the novel as a source of immorality, he would most likely view the novel's death with some kind of satisfaction.

21. D (Scope: *Paragraph 3*)
The 3rd paragraph describes a connection between people's reaction to the album with the rise of digitalized music and the possible similar fate of the novel. Thus the correct answer must contain the ideas of "people", "music" and "novels".

22. A (Scope: *Lines 41-47*)
These lines contrast the computer screen's lack of "feeling" and "interaction" (line 42-43) with the book's interactive nature. So the primary distinction is between disconnection (computer screens) and engagement (books).

23. D (Scope: *Line 51*)
The context shows that the term "conveyance" has to do with the communication of ideas between a book and its reader. In this context, "transmittance" is the best fit.

24. E (Scope: *Paragraphs 4 and 5*)
The assertion is summarized in lines 39-41, while the citation (quote) occurs in lines 54-58.

Section 2

1. A (commonplace...esoteric)
  normal...strange

(B) anomalous...eccentric
  different...odd
(C) cerebral...discordant
  smart...dislike
(D) resolute...listless
  brave...indifferent
(E) incredulous...trenchant
  questioning...relevant

2. D (acumen...resolute)
  smart...brave

(A) beneficence...covetous
  generous...greedy
(B) delineation...fraudulent
  to explain...false
(C) vacuity...germane
  stupid...relevant
(E) liberality...conventional
  generous...normal

3. B (advocates: *argue for*)

(A) empathizes: *feeling*
(C) belies: *misrepresent*
(D) discloses: *share*
(E) amasses: *gather*

4. C (inclusive: *including*)

(A) antagonistic: *hate*
(B) ephemera: *short-lived*
(D) innate: *in-born*
(E) eclectic: *different*

5. B (homogeneous: *same*)

(A) reticent: *shy*
(C) ephemeral: *short-lived*
(D) pervasive: *widespread*
(E) specious: *false*

6. E (Scope: *Passage 1*)
The main ideas of Passage 1 are "media" and "fear", a fact that allows you to eliminate choices (A), (B), and (D). Choice (C) incorrectly blames the media for the fear.

7. E (Scope: *Passage 2*)
The author of Passage 2 blames the media (lines 15-16 & 21-24). This negative tone is only present in choices (E) and (C), and "indignation" is too strongly negative to be correct.

8. C (Scope: *Passages 1 and 2*)
Agreement questions for double passages are like main idea questions. The main ideas of Passages 1 and 2 are "media" and "fear", a fact that allows you to eliminate choices (A), (B), and (D). Choice (E) incorrectly includes the idea of "benefit", which is not present in either passage.

9. C (Scope: *Passages 1 and 2*)
An authority ("psychologist") is cited in lines 11-13. Neither author includes choices (A), (B), (C), or (D).

10. E (Scope: *Line 9*)
The assertion ("It's a natural progression") is followed by examples of mines and mining.

11. E (Scope: *Lines 6-8*)
Only this choice contains the main ideas of "the middle class" (line 5) and resources such as "copper, iron, and zinc" (line 8).

12. B (Scope: *Lines 10-15*)
These lines describe the formation of, and thus account for the presence of, minerals in the ocean.

13. D (Scope: *Line 25*)
In the passage, the word "addresses" is linked with "previous injustices". Only "deals with" fits this context.

14. D (Scope: *Lines 22-25*)
Only this choice holds the central ideas of the lines: "terrestrial mining" (line 19) and "indigenous societies" (line 22).

15. C (Scope: *Lines 38-40*)
Undermine means to weaken the argument. If the industry itself paid for the study that makes underwater mining easier by claiming that there are few species, this fact would cast serious doubt on the study.

16. C (Scope: *Line 40*)
Coming after the phrase "harsh conditions" (lines 39-40), the phrase "far from the light of the sun" serves to emphasize or punctuate the preceding phrase.

17. A (Scope: *Line 6*)
The context sentence contrasts the idea of "vigor" with that of "restraint". Since "restraint" has a connotation of being subdued, the best antonym is "enthusiasm".

18. C (Scope: *Lines 7-9*)
The fact that the people cross the street when they see the narrator coming hints at the fact that they do not like him, as they actively make clear.

19. D (Scope: *Lines 25-27*)
Only this choice contains the lines' key idea, the three poems, and the person of Crump.

20. D (Scope: *Line 33*)
Crump's increasing efforts to avoid contact with the narrator make it clear that Crump has no knowledge of any

21. E (Scope: *Lines 34-46*)
Since the narrator mistakenly believes that there is an agreement between him and Crump, the narrator continues to misread Crump's actions. These include changing his phone number and building the fence.

22. E (Scope: *Lines 48-49*)
In context, the shift occurs precisely in the wake of Crump extending the fence between the two properties.

23. B (Scope: *Whole Passage*)
All of Crump's actions in the passage imply that he is frustrated or irritated. These actions include changing his phone number, building the fence, and going on vacation.

24. D (Scope: *Whole Passage*)

In the passage, Crump tries repeatedly to avoid all contact with the author. Given that and the fact that the vacation has already lasted more than nine months, it can be safely inferred that Crump has no intention of ever returning.

Section 3

1. E (apprehension...pauperize)
   afraid...poor

(A) insolvency...deceive
   poor...lying
(B) iconoclasm...rebuff
   odd   to argue against
(C) extravagance...malign
   rich...to insult
(D) bewilderment...invalidate
   confused...to argue against

2. E (prevalent: *widespread*)

(A) inclusive: *including*
(B) similar: *alike*
(C) ephemeral: *short-lived*
(D) spurious: *false*

3. C (aberration…magnanimity)
  different…generous

(A) munificence…gluttony
  generous…greedy
(B) toady…uniformity
  to flatter…same
(D) parody…perplexity
  mocking…confused
(E) chastisement…prodigality
  to scold…rich

4. C (specious…indubitable)
  false…true

(A) lavish…excursive
  rich…irrelevant
(B) covert…apt
  secretive…secretive
(D) eccentric…remunerative
  odd…rich
(E) lukewarm…mendacious
  indifferent…lying

5. B (arbitrary: *irrelevant / random*)

(A) eclectic: *different / odd*
(C) sage: *smart*
(D) inherent: *in-born*
(E) homogeneous: *same*

6. E (proliferation: *a lot*)

(A) exclusiveness: *not shared*
(B) antipathy: *hate*
(C) documentation: *record*
(D) reticence: *shy*

7. E (Scope: *Lines 3-7*)
The lines make a distinction between honest alchemists and "charlatans" (line 5).

8. A (Scope: *Whole Passage*)
Only this choice correctly identifies the two key ideas of the passage: "alchemists" and "chemistry".

9. B (Scope: *Line 3*)
In the context sentence, "invention"(line 2) is used as a synonym for "devise", so "create" is the best definition.

10. E (Scope: *Lines 11-14*)
In these lines, "these countries" refers to "several countries". The author also makes a connection between the attitudes of people in these countries and the play, *R.U.R.*

11. E (Scope: *Lines 1-4*)
The referenced lines refer to the contrast between the American scientists, who received little notice, and American artists. This contrast implies that the artists received attention.

12. B (Scope: *Line 16*)
In the context sentence, the idea is that the universities felt that their time and resources were not ultimately worth it. Thus "worthwhile" is the best definition.

13. E (Scope: *Line 36*)
The "dark shadows" are a contrast of Julian's new liberties in Vienna (lines 30-35). Thus the implication is that, before his move to Vienna, he suffered prejudice like that detailed in lines 12-20.

14. C (Scope: *Line 43*)
Since the context sentence mentions the colleagues' "pervasive racism", the quotation marks serve to accentuate the distance between Just and the others.

15. C (Scope: *Line 48-51*)
The idea addressed is cellular holism, which states that an organism can't be explained by its parts but only by the interaction of its parts. Since the active interaction of the parts is most important, choice (C) is the best answer.

16. E (Scope: *Whole Passage*)
The entire passage deals with two Black scientists, Julian and Just. Only choice (E) contains both figures.

17. B (Scope: *Line 59*)
In context, "range" is used in the familiar sense of scope. Only "gamut" fits this definition.

18. D (Scope: *Lines 65-68*)
In these lines, the author compares the present with the past and casts a skeptical eye on the idea of progress having been made. Thus "cynicism" best describes the author's tone.

19. E (Scope: *Lines 61-63*)

Only choice (E) contains all three of the key ideas contained in the lines: Just, biologists, and approach.

SAT CRITICAL READING PRACTICE TEST 4

Time: 20 Minutes
19 Questions

> **Directions:** Choose the answer that is grammatically correct, concise, and unambiguous.

1. Mrs. Dillard was no mere ----- in the area of antique pickles; indeed, she was renowned, far and wide, as an expert.

(A) sage   (B) eccentric   (C) dilettante
      (D) pacifist   (E) advocate

2. In spite of his ----- protests otherwise, it was clear from his twitchy eyes and sweaty palms that he was ----- the prospect of fighting sharks.

(A) insatiable…nonchalant about
(B) open-handed…furtive about
(C) ardent…daunted by
(D) apocryphal…covetous of
(E) tremulous…undaunted by

3. Fenster was ----- in his reaction to the police, answering only with sarcasm and insults.

(A) affable   (B) flippant   (C) gregarious
      (D) reticent   (E) elusive

4. She remained ----- in her beliefs about Christmas decorations, mercilessly squashing any opinions that differed from her own.

(A) exhaustive   (B) erroneous   (C) dogmatic
      (D) bleak   (E) conciliatory

5. Forced to attend a lame concert, Billy ----- his unkind fate to anyone who would listen.

(A) lamented   (B) condoned   (C) mollified
      (D) expedited   (E) bolstered

6. The teacher gave the student's homework a ----- glance, returning it after only a few seconds.

(A) contracting   (B) misanthropic   (C) cursory
      (D) multitudinous   (E) conciliatory

7. A fine line exists between -----, the hoarding of money without necessity, and sensibility, the saving of money to prevent future -----.

(A) fidelity…insolvency
(B) intrepidness…amalgamation
(C) miserliness…indigence
(D) inscrutability…remuneration
(E) vapidity…discord

8. Science operates on the premise that no theory is -----, and any theory can be overturned by an astute, ----- insight bolstered by facts.

(A) digressive…doltish
(B) incontrovertible…ingenious
(C) magnanimous…anomalous
(D) remunerative…mendacious
(E) obsequious…pusillanimous

Questions 9-19 are based on the following passage.

"I don't remember what I did last week."
This phrase normally incurs dread when issued
from the lips of two groups: children and the
elderly. For the latter group, in particular, the
5   inability to remember details is seen as a
failing or as a symptom of inevitable mental
decline. While imperfect recall points toward a
grave condition in some cases, it may actually
represent an advantage for the older population
10   at large.
    A distinction must be made between the
types of memory involved. Each person
possesses a kind of long-term memory called
explicit memory which records the pertinent
15   specifics of a person's life. Explicit memory is
comprised of autobiographical memory, which
records specific details, and semantic memory,
which attempts to generalize from these
experiences.
20   As I write this line, I cannot recall driving
home from work last week. My reason tells
me, that since I made it home, I must have
driven there. Yet my memory has not stored
any of the details of this particular situation. In
25   fact, it would be a waste of my mental capacity
to remember such an event, because all the
prior experiences of 24 years of driving the
same route have been generalized. The
efficiency of my semantic memory has
30   superseded the necessity for my
autobiographical memory to record the
particulars of every single event in which I
drive home.
    Seen in the light of adaptation for survival,
35   this arrangement makes sense. Autobiographical memory is necessary in order to
process new stimuli, such as those with which
children are constantly encountering. As
previous encounters multiply and accumulate,
40   however, the necessity to remember the details
of each particular situation diminishes. Instead,
generalizations from prior experiences can be
utilized in order to handle the manifestation of
any subsequent similar situation. Therefore, as
45   time passes, memory becomes more semantic
and less autobiographical.
    In the case of the elderly, what is often
sloppily referred to as "memory loss" may in
fact be an example of adaptation. Because

50   one's store of experiences expands with time,
one does not need to squander precious mental
resources recording redundant and unhelpful
information. In this fashion, memory loss may
in fact be memory gain.
55   So the next time you interact with an older
person, including me, do not be so quick to
judge an inability to recollect a recent event as
a weakness. It may, in fact, represent a strength
that is on the verge of apprehension.

9. In line 2, the word "dread" most nearly means

(A) reverence
(B) trepidation
(C) admiration
(D) awe
(E) astonishment

10. In lines 8-10, the author primarily offers

(A) an enigmatic contradiction
(B) an apathetic assessment
(C) a colorful digression
(D) a frank criticism
(E) a surprising contention

11. In lines 20-33, the author primarily

(A) recounts an autobiographical memory
(B) debunks the idea of semantic memory
(C) criticizes her own lack of memory
(D) extends an instance of semantic memory
(E) offers an autobiographical example

12. In line 8, the word "grave" most nearly means

(A) momentous
(B) somber
(C) dark
(D) serious
(E) important

13. Lines 35-38 chiefly suggests that

(A) stimuli are necessary for the formation of
    autobiographical memory
(B) children do not possess semantic memory
(C) autobiographical memory processes novel
    experiences
(D) memory steadily diminishes over time
(E) the elderly do not need autobiographical memory

14. The 5th paragraph primarily serves to

(A) affront those who suffer from memory loss
(B) clarify the process of memory making
(C) demonstrate that what is commonly thought to
    be a weakness is actually a strength
(D) point out that the elderly often waste their
    mental capabilities
(E) show the difference between loss and gain

15. In line 51, the word "precious" most nearly
means

(A) invaluable
(B) beloved
(C) artificial
(D) thoroughgoing
(E) affected

16. In lines 55-58, the author primarily implies that

(A) she often interacts with the memories of the
    elderly
(B) all elderly persons are unable to recall recent
    events
(C) autobiographical memory is often used by the
    elderly
(D) she is an elderly woman herself
(E) semantic memory is the sole resource available
    to the elderly

17. Lines 15-19 primarily state that

(A) two distinct types of memory make up explicit
    memory
(B) autobiographical memory is responsible for
    generalizing memories
(C) people rely more heavily on semantic memory
(D) specific details of experience are the foundation
    of explicit memory
(E) explicit memory weakens as a person ages

18. Lines 35-38 primarily imply that

(A) adults have no need for autobiographical
    memory
(B) autobiographical memory ensures that a people
    do not need to remember every detail of their
    lives
(C) children rely heavily on autobiographical
    memory
(D) new stimuli could not exist without
    autobiographical memory
(E) the elderly often do not recall events

19. In line 58 , the word "strength" primarily refers
to

(A) processing of new stimuli
(B) imperfect recall
(C) generalization of experience
(D) mental capacity
(E) autobiographical memory

END SECTION

Time: 25 Minutes
24 Questions

Directions: Choose the answer that is grammatically correct, concise, and unambiguous.

1. The city was unprepared when the ----- danger of hurricanes became reality, bringing destructive waves that ----- everything in their path.

(A) ambivalent…detracted
(B) profound…assuaged
(C) colloquial…supplanted
(D) hypothetical…obliterated
(E) illicit…delineated

2. Stalin had such ----- appetite for ornate statues that his advisors were panicked by the potential appearance of voracity and ----- on his part.

(A) a ravenous…rapacity
(B) a meager…liberality
(C) a spurious…indigence
(D) an amorous…eccentricity
(E) an esoteric…listlessness

3. Duane jumped into the pool immediately after lunch, determined to ----- the idea that one must wait 30 minutes between eating and swimming.

(A) concede   (B) placate   (C) dupe
     (D) debunk   (E) rectify

4. Not content with mere speech, she brought along charts and graphs to ----- her arguments.

(A) concede   (B) coax   (C) acknowledge
     (D) sanction   (E) bolster

5. After more combative approaches failed, the company took a ----- stance in its negotiations.

(A) flagrant (B) precarious (C) transient
     (D) conciliatory   (E) misanthropic

Questions 6-9 are based on the following passages.

Passage 1

An exploration of genetically-modified crops must be based upon the facts, quite apart from primordial fears of "unnatural" interventions in nature. Common food crops
5   have been genetically modified through selection for hundreds of years. Gregor Mendel, for example, extensively modified the pea to express desirable traits, and yet no environmental or religious groups decry the
10 pea as "Frankenfood". The truth is that genetic engineering allows for significant improvements in seed crops, such as decreased germination times and enlarged crop yields. These improvements have already enhanced
15 the nutrition and the lives of thousands. The only obstacle to similarly advancing the lives of millions more of the impoverished is not capability but rather apprehension.

Passage 2

Shrill denunciations of genetically-
20 engineered crops undermine the efforts of movements opposed to such crops. Several legitimate reasons exist for the delay, or even the stoppage, of the introduction of modified crops. Because these crops have been studied
25 for only a brief time, their long-term environmental impact remains unknown. It may be that they pose a threat not only to native plants, as seems to already have happened in some North African countries, but
30 that they also pose a grave hazard to human health. Until these concerns are mollified through rigorous scientific study, it remains unwise, and potentially devastating, to rush to exploit the potential benefits of these crops.

6. In line 30, the word "hazard" most nearly means

(A) luck
(B) obstacle
(C) danger
(D) gamble
(E) guess

7. In Passage 2, the attitude of the author towards genetically-engineered crops can best be described as

(A) cautious optimism
(B) harsh derision
(C) mild perplexity
(D) complete awe
(E) resigned frustration

8. The authors of Passage 1 and Passage 2 would most likely agree that

(A) Gregor Mendel originated the genetic modification of crops
(B) the augmentation of crop yields and food supplies guarantees the improvement of human lives
(C) scientists are not yet certain of the long-term environmental effects of engineered crops
(D) the objections of those people opposed to genetically-engineered crops are baseless
(E) the introduction of genetically-engineered crops may ultimately prove valuable

9. The author of Passage 2 would most likely respond to the argument in lines 15-18 by

(A) dismissing the severity of the lives of the poor
(B) advocating the use of native seeds and crops
(C) reiterating the necessity for higher crop yields
(D) suspecting the nutritional value of crops
(E) accentuating the validity of fear

Questions 10-16 are based on the following passage.

The circumstances of what became known as "Nat Turner's rebellion" are corroborated by history. On August 21, 1831, a small group of slaves began an insurrection in Southampton,
5   Virginia with the killing of the Turner family. The rebels proceeded to kill approximately 57 white men, women, and children over the course of two days, before the state militia thwarted the rebellion. In the wake of these
10   events, some 200 Black people were killed, many of whom had no involvement in the rebellion.

Before these events only "Nat" had existed. Nat was born on October 2nd, 1800 in
15   the household of Benjamin Turner and given a single name. In 1831, Nat was sold to Joseph Travis. In the wake of the failed rebellion that year, Nat went into hiding and lastly hid in a cave near the Turner residence. On October 30,
20   Nat emerged from the cave without resistance and was taken to the local courthouse, where the paltry sum of these autobiographical facts would be subsumed into the character of "Nat Turner".

25   If Thomas Ruffin Gray did not coin the name "Nat Turner", he nonetheless created the character behind the name. For Gray, a white slave-owner and lawyer who had been appointed by the court to represent Nat, took it
30   upon himself to create the narrative, *The Confessions of Nat Turner*. The Nat Turner of its pages is a volatile mixture of stereotype, misguided religious lunacy, and calm bloodthirstiness. In short, Nat Turner is nothing
35   more than the reflection of the biases and fears, and the reflexive necessity to allay these fears, of the author and of his society.

Since that initial narrative, which sold more than 50,000 copies in its day, Nat Turner
40   has become a favored character of writers. At least six novels have been published, across more than 150 years, which take him as the central character. They have all portrayed him in radically disparate lights, rushing in to
45   invent the details and motivations that history cannot give. Each, in its own way, is a brilliant failure that mirrors the spectacular failures of race relations.

Nat Turner has never existed as a man and
50   will never exist, except as a ghostly figure that each era resurrects for the haunting that suits it best.

10. The 1st paragraph primarily serves to

(A) supply statistical support for a thesis
(B) broach the character of Nat Turner
(C) perpetuate a common legacy
(D) offer the accepted history of an insurrection
(E) denounce the injustices of slavery

11. Lines 13-14 primarily represent

(A) an audacious thesis that refutes accepted opinion
(B) a transition from broad history to personal history
(C) an elegiac note for the dead of the rebellion
(D) a sober reassessment of a previous opinion
(E) a shift to the consequences of the insurrection

12. In line 22, the word "paltry" most nearly means

(A) negligible
(B) base
(C) cheap
(D) shoddy
(E) rotten

13. Based on the passage, Gray is chiefly responsible for

(A) prosecuting Nat Turner at his criminal trial
(B) engendering racial prejudices within his society
(C) advertising the popularity of his writings
(D) propagating religious lunacy and bloodthirstiness
(E) composing the persona of Nat Turner

14. Lines 34-37 primarily suggest that

(A) prejudices are always created by society
(B) Gray portrayed Turner, not as a man, but as an embodiment of alarm and its comfort
(C) Gray failed to extinguish the trepidation within his readers
(D) Turner was a figure of terror to his society
(E) Gray heightened the grimness of his narrative in order to sell more copies

15. The author mentions the "six novels" (line 41) primarily to

(A) confirm the veracity of Gray's *Confessions*
(B) denounce the disparities in the characters of Nat Turner that the novels present
(C) adulate the inventiveness of their authors
(D) acclaim the pervasive popularity of their narratives
(E) highlight the invented nature of Nat Turner

16. The conclusion of the author in lines 49-52 can best be described as

(A) spiteful
(B) presumptuous
(C) matter-of-fact
(D) nonchalant
(E) rancorous

Questions 17-24 are based on the following passage.

The story of the internment of Japanese-Americans is often assumed to end on January 2, 1945. This date marked the revocation of the emergency internment order and the official
5   closure of the camps. On this day, all *Issei*, those people born in Japan, and *Nisei*, those people born in the United States of Japanese parents, were ostensibly free and enthusiastically encouraged to return "home".
10   Yet, a full five months later, only 57,000 of the 112,000 Japanese-Americans confined in the camps had actually left them.

Many Japanese-Americans who remained cited fear of their treatment as the primary
15   reason for not returning to their previous homes. As one man interned at the Manzanar barracks in California said, "I would like to take my people back home but there are too many people in Los Angeles who would resent
20   our return." This concern was not unfounded, as twenty-four violent incidents against Japanese-Americans had been reported on the West Coast since the closing of the camps, with many more incidents probably remaining
25   unreported. Yet fear of intimidation or violence did not represent the foremost reason for the extended residence in camps.

Most Japanese-Americans, simply put, had nothing left in their hometowns. In the frenzied
30   48 hours between the notice of internment and the required registration at assembly centers, many Japanese-Americans had sold their homes and businesses. Others had maintained their home but had their business equipment
35   requisitioned by the government or stolen by looters. Compounded by the shortage of available laborers, this lack of equipment made business virtually impossible for those who did return to their hometowns from detention.
40   While some of the interned did return to Japan following the end of World War II, most eventually returned to their previous homes on the West coast or resettled in the Midwest. And still the story of the internment has yet to
45   conclude. In the words of one man, who was interned as a teenager, "I've been telling this story since I left the service and I'll be telling it for 50 more years if that's what it takes."

17. The first paragraph primarily serves to

(A) proffer a timeline of World War II
(B) invoke Japanese-American witness statements
(C) define key terms in the argument
(D) elicit an emotional response to internment
(E) provide historical background

18. Based on the passage, the author most likely places the word "home" (line 9) in quotation marks to

(A) rebut the domestic arrangements of the internment camps
(B) underscore the bafflement caused by the word
(C) endorse the idea that any dwelling can be a home
(D) reinforce the ambiguity of the word at the time
(E) point out the housing surplus in the U.S.

19. In line 14, the word "primary" most nearly means

(A) essential
(B) chief
(C) primitive
(D) preliminary
(E) firsthand

20. According to the passage, the phrase "'my people'" (line 18) most likely refers to

(A) *Issei* who wanted to repatriate to Japan
(B) teenagers interned at the camps
(C) *Nisei* who served overseas in the war
(D) laborers for farm work and for other businesses
(E) family members interned at the camp

21. Lines 17-20 primarily imply that

(A) Los Angeles was a center of prejudice against
　　　Japanese-Americans
(B) the internees at the Manzanar camp were
　　　particularly apprehensive about leaving
(C) news of the abuse of departed Japanese-
　　　Americans reached the internment camps
(D) the majority of those on the West Coast
　　　welcomed back the Japanese-Americans
(E) the man quoted preferred to return to Japan
　　　rather than to Los Angeles

22. According to the passage, the "shortage of available laborers" (line 36-37) was most likely due to

(A) the rapid execution of the internment order
(B) the expanded military of World War II
(C) the sparse population of the Midwest
(D) the return of most Japanese-Americans to Japan
(E) the low birth rate during World War II

23. Lines 46-48 primarily imply that

(A) teenagers represented the majority of interned
　　　Japanese-Americans
(B) the quoted man had also refused to immediately
　　　leave an internment camp in 1945
(C) the story of Japanese-American internment has
　　　yet to be fully apprehended
(D) *Nisei* adjusted to post-war life more smoothly
　　　than did *Issei*
(E) the quoted man is tired of telling the story after
　　　recounting it for 50 years

24. In line 33, the word "maintained" most likely means

(A) asserted
(B) wielded
(C) defended
(D) observed
(E) kept

END SECTION

Time: 25 Minutes
24 Questions

Directions: Choose the answer that is grammatically correct, concise, and unambiguous.

1. Kathy's friends ultimately decided that her assertion that rocks make good pets was -----; it relied solely on a faulty and ----- argument.

(A) inscrutable…jaded
(B) conventional…craven
(C) invalid…fallacious
(D) eccentric…laudatory
(E) penurious…rancorous

2. His appearance was generally -----; he rarely combed his hair, brushed his teeth, or washed his clothes.

(A) bleak   (B) anomalous   (C) exhaustive
    (D) unkempt   (E) flagrant

3. The con man employed his strange, ----- charm and gift for speech in order to ----- lonely old women out of their life savings.

(A) disparaging…commend
(B) apathetic…rebuke
(C) eccentric…exalt
(D) tangential…abound
(E) quixotic…dupe

4. Only after a long, ----- chat about the weather on Mars did the CEO broach the ----- point: the impending insolvency of the company

(A) amorous…aberrant
(B) dubious…indubitable
(C) impecunious…prodigal
(D) arcane…commendable
(E) discursive…pertinent

5. In their designs, builders must account for the tendency of concrete to ----- in cold weather.

(A) bolster   (B) obscure   (C) contract
    (D) affirm   (E) diverge

6. While skipping over words that you don't know is certainly -----, it will not help you to increase your vocabulary.

(A) cursory   (B) implausible   (C) unwarranted
    (D) expedient   (E) esoteric

Questions 7-8 are based on the following passage.

According to the ninth annual Lemelson-MIT Invention Index study, over thirty percent of adults in the U.S. claim that the cell phone is the one invention they hate the most. While
5 cellular mobile phones have existed since the early seventies, they only recently became a worldwide commodity.

Nowadays almost everyone across the globe, from the elderly in Brazil to young
10 children in Switzerland, can be found with a cellular device of some sort. Perhaps while cell phones do serve a practical purpose to the customers that use them, we have forgotten that only two decades ago ninety-five percent
15 of the world's population was without one.

Perhaps today more than one-third of American adults "despise" the cell phone because we have become so utterly dependent on it.

7. In the passage, Americans' attitude toward cell phones can best be described as

(A) unabashedly approving
(B) grudgingly accepting
(C) openly hostile
(D) solemnly respectful
(E) generally nostalgic

8. The primary purpose of the passage is to

(A) denounce the expanded use of cell phones around the world
(B) discuss the practical purposes of cell phones
(C) defend American's ambivalent relationship with cell phones
(D) condemn the dependence of Americans on cell phones
(E) examine Americans' attitudes towards cell phones

Questions 9-10 are based on the following passage.

While the concept of cellular communication dates back to the late nineteen-forties, Dr. Martin Cooper, a former manager at Motorola, put the first portable handset to
5 use in 1973. Originally, the idea for modern cell phones began when Bell Lab researchers worked on a makeshift mobile car phone. They realized that by applying small cells with frequency reuse, they could increase the traffic
10 capacity of mobile phones. However, during that time the necessary technology to generate such cellular activity had yet to be created. Then, after various trials and errors in the late sixties and early seventies, Dr. Cooper was
15 able to increase frequency allocation just enough to make a call on his own makeshift cellular phone. The first person he called was his rival, Joel Engel, at Bell Labs.

9. In lines 9-10, the author implies that Dr. Cooper is

(A) technologically savvy
(B) generally indifferent
(C) extremely ambitious
(D) greatly competitive
(E) condescendingly rude

10. The passage can best be described as a

(A) chronological list of events in the history of cellular activity
(B) personal anecdote on the trials of Dr. Martin Cooper
(C) brief history of the invention of the first cell phone
(D) general history of Bell Labs
(E) short story about the practicality of modern cell phones

Questions 11-16 are based on the following passage.

A visit to your local library will no doubt confirm the preciseness with which the books are catalogued. A further trip to a bookstore will vindicate the idea that the classification of
5 books has reached an apex of efficiency and speed in the readers' ability to retrieve the books. This system works brilliantly, if the reader knows precisely what title, author, or subject matter she desires.
10   The problem arises for those who are uncertain of what book they would like to read. These stout, gallant souls must wander into a bookstore and then make a sort of Hobson's choice between fiction and non-fiction.
15   If they select fiction, they are forced into the chaos that lies beneath the seeming order of titles arranged by authors' last names. Browsers stand before shelves in the vain endeavor to make a connection between titles
20 by "Adame" and "Adams" beyond mere alphabetic chance. And so it goes from "A" to "Z", through novels and poetry.

If the seeking readers select non-fiction, they almost immediately confront a second
25 choice. Now, they must select from a series of classes and subject matter, such as "History", "Religion", and "Philosophy". This organized ambiguity seems to entertain the promise of interaction, with disparate subjects crammed
30 up against each other on the shelves, until perusing readers discover the dominion of nonsensical sub-classes such as "English Philosophy".

At a time of an unprecedented number of
35 books, necessity now dictates that libraries and bookstores are designed for the reader who searches not for the expected, but the unexpected. In these spaces, perhaps books could be arranged by theme. Imagine walking
40 into a bookstore and discovering a section for "Journeys to the Underworld". Imagine the astonishing interactions as you browsed between the known and the unknown of *The Divine Comedy* and "The Legend of Zhong
45 Kui", of *The Aeneid* and "The Legend of Hun Hunahpu". Imagine listening to the Florentine and the Chinese, the Roman and the Maya conversing with one another through time. I hear them now. Imagine hearing them, too.

11. The main idea of the passage is

(A) the current organization of books at libraries and bookstores
(B) the difficulty of choosing between fiction and non-fiction books
(C) the requirement for a novel approach to the organization of books
(D) the impracticality of arranging books in alphabetical order
(E) the efficiency of the current book classification system

12. The attitude of the author towards the current "classification of books" (line 4-5) can best be described as

(A) ambivalent
(B) confounded
(C) scornful
(D) jaded
(E) incredulous

13. In line 12, the word "stout" most nearly means

(A) bold
(B) strong
(C) bulky
(D) forceful
(E) stubborn

14. In lines 27-30, the author primarily implies that

(A) English Philosophy is not a valid classification
(B) crowded bookshelves are inherently interactive
(C) non-fiction books should be organized in alphabetical order
(D) ambiguity is the ideal organizing principle
(E) interaction should be the goal in the organization of books

15. Lines 34-38 can best be categorized as

(A) a denunciation
(B) a call to action
(C) an apology
(D) a concession
(E) a parody

16. In lines 38-46, the author primarily assumes that

(A) the cited stories are present in every bookstore
(B) non-fiction can be grouped with fiction
(C) stories of differing languages can be understood
(D) books can be arranged thematically
(E) readers would prefer to have new sections within
        bookstores

Questions 17-24 are based on the following passage.

A recent travel show featured the Great
Pyramid at Giza in Egypt, the statues of Easter
Island in the south Pacific, and the city of
Tiahuanaco in Bolivia. During the program, the
5   host categorized these ancient constructions as
geographically disparate but thematically
united as great achievements. While this
opinion is certainly legitimate, it does not
cover the full spectrum of what these
10 architectural wonders share.

In fact, their very existence has been
attributed to the inspiration and ingenuity of
the lost people of Atlantis, to vanished races of
benevolent giants, and even to extraterrestrial
15 beings. Advocates of these views may lie on
the periphery of modern archaeology, but they
stand firmly in a long line of tradition. Their
ideas may seem laughably harmless, or even
entertaining, except that they sustain the worst
20 aspects of paternalism and prejudice.

The city of Tiahuanaco stands more than
12,500 feet above sea level, making it the
highest major city to ever exist. The great city
was abandoned by the time that the Spanish
25 *conquistadors* arrived in the region in the mid-
16th century. When questioned by the
Spaniards as to the builders of such a
remarkable city, the Aymara Indians who now
lived in the region could only answer that it
30 had been people who had lived before the Inca.
Unable to credit the predecessors of these
"lowly" people with such a magnificent
endeavor, the Spanish soon theorized that a
vanished race of giants had built Tihuanaca.

35 Nothing had changed this view by the 19th
century, when the city became a travel
destination for rich, privileged Europeans. The
accounts of these travelers are remarkably
similarly in hailing the city and in speculating
40 that the builders of Tihuanaca must have been
civilized in the "old World" and then
disappeared suddenly without time to transmit
their knowledge to the local people. The apex
of such theories was perhaps put forth by Thor
45 Heyerdahl, who advocated the idea that a white
and bearded race, dubbed the *Viracochas*, had
built Tihuanaca and then moved on.

While this particular theory has been
discredited by later writers, and the
50 propagation of such explicitly racial theories is
now considered impolitic, the urge to deny the
ingenuity and the splendor of Tihuanaca to its
rightful heirs persists. Perhaps even more
disturbingly, the modern "explanations" of the
55 city's construction, both those that posit a lost
race and those that engage an extraterrestrial
one, continue to find an accepting audience
that numbers in the millions.

17. Lines 11-15 primarily serve to

(A) introduce key terms
(B) discredit an opposing viewpoint
(C) expand upon a previous point
(D) endorse a common opinion
(E) highlight an architectural fallacy

18. Lines 17-20 primarily suggest that

(A) archaeological theories involving outlandish
      scenarios are amusing
(B) *conquistadors* started a tradition of prejudice
      that remains in place today
(C) some current archaeological thought continues to
      espouse discrimination
(D) the origins of ancient architecture is a harsh
      enigma that may never be solved
(E) the citizens of Tihuanaco abandoned the city in
      the face of bigotry

19. In line 32, the author most likely places
quotation marks around the word "lowly" in order to

(A) corroborate the opinion held by the Spanish
(B) punctuate the ignorance of the Aymara regarding
      the constructors of Tihuanaca
(C) satirize the idea that giants had built Tihuanaca
(D) reinforce the disparity between the low status of
      the Aymara and the grandeur of Tihuanaca
(E) dispute the estimation of the Aymara by the
      Spaniards

20. In line 39, the word "hailing" most nearly means

(A) welcoming
(B) precipitating
(C) praising
(D) falling
(E) confirming

21. The attitude of the author towards "rich, privileged Europeans" (line 37) can best be described as

(A) scornfully derisive
(B) mildly appreciative
(C) perfectly nonchalant
(D) principally critical
(E) slightly dumbfounded

22. According to the passage, the "old World" (line 41) would most likely be located in which of the following countries?

(A) Bolivia
(B) China
(C) Egypt
(D) Spain
(F) Australia

23. According to the passage, the "rightful heirs" (line 53) would most likely be the

(A) Easter Islanders
(B) Spaniards
(C) Bolivians
(D) Amayra Indians
(E) Viracochas

24. In line 56, the word "engage" most nearly means

(A) promise
(B) attract
(C) occupy
(D) use
(E) participate

END SECTION

Practice Test 4
Answer Key and Explanations

Section1

1. C
2. C
3. B
4. C
5. A
6. C
7. C
8. B
9. B
10. E
11. D
12. D
13. C
14. C
15. A
16. D
17. A
18. C
19. C

Section 2

1. D
2. A
3. D
4. E
5. D
6. C
7. A
8. E
9. E
10. D
11. B
12. A
13. E
14. B

15. E
16. C
17. E
18. D
19. B
20. E
21. C
22. B
23. C
24. E

Section 3

1. C
2. D
3. E
4. E
5. C
6. D
7. B
8. E
9. D
10. C
11. D
12. A
13. A
14. E
15. B
16. D
17. C
18. C
19. E
20. C
21. D
22. D
23. D
24. D

Finding Your Score

Raw score: Total Number Right – [Total Number Wrong ÷ 4] = _____

Notes: 1) Omissions are not counted towards your raw score
         2) If the total number wrong ÷ 4 ends in .5 or .75, it is rounded up

Critical Reading Scoring Table

Raw Score	Scaled Score	Raw Score	Scaled Score
67	800	32	540
66	800	31	530
65	800	30	520
64	800	29	520
63	780	28	510
62	770	27	500
61	760	26	500
60	740	25	490
59	730	24	480
58	720	23	470
57	710	22	460
56	700	21	460
55	690	20	450
54	680	19	440
53	670	18	430
52	660	17	430
51	660	16	420
50	650	15	420
49	640	14	400
48	630	13	390
47	630	12	380
46	620	11	370
45	610	10	370
44	610	9	360
43	600	8	350
42	590	7	340
41	590	6	330
40	580	5	320
39	580	4	310
38	570	3	300
37	560	2	280
36	560	1	260
35	550	0	240
34	550	-1	220
33	540	-2	200

Strength and Weakness Review

Go back to the test and circle the questions that you answered incorrectly. This review will allow you to see what answer explanations to study more closely for problem-solving techniques. It will also allow you to see what question types and passage types you need to review more carefully.

	Section 1	Section 2	Section 3
Passage Types			
Aesthetics / Arts			11-16
Biography		10-16	
Fiction			
History		17-24	9-10
Hard Sciences	9-19	6-9	
Social Sciences			7-8, 17-24
Question Types			
Assumption			16
Attitude / Tone		7, 16	7, 12, 21
Inference	13, 16, 18	9, 14, 15, 18, 20, 21, 22, 23	9, 14, 18, 19, 22, 23
Literal Comprehension	10, 11, 14, 17, 19	8, 10, 11, 13, 17	15
Main Idea			10, 11
Primary Purpose			8
Structure			
Word-in-Context	12, 15	6, 12, 19, 24	13, 20, 24

Section 1

1. C (dilettante: *amateur*)

(A) sage: *smart*
(B) eccentric: *different / odd*
(D) pacifist: *make better*
(E) advocate: *argue for*

2. C (ardent...daunted by)
  passionate...afraid

(A) insatiable...nonchalant about
  greedy...indifferent
(B) open-handed...furtive about
  generous...secretive
(D) apocryphal...covetous of
  false...greedy
(E) tremulous...undaunted by
  afraid...brave

3. B (flippant: *disrespectful*)

(A) affable: *friendly*
(C) gregarious: *friendly*
(D) reticent: *shy*
(E) elusive: *avoid*

4. C (dogmatic: *stubborn*)

(A) exhaustive: *thorough*
(B) erroneous: *error*
(D) bleak: *depressed*
(E) conciliatory: *friendly*

5. A (lamented: *mourn*)

(B) condoned: *approve*
(C) mollified: *make better*
(D) expedited: *sped up*
(E) bolstered: *argue for*

6. C (cursory: *short-lived*)

(A) contracting: *make small*
(B) misanthropic: *hate*
(D) multitudinous: *a lot*
(E) conciliatory: *friendly*

7. C (miserliness...indigence)
  greedy...poor

(A) fidelity...insolvency
  true...poor
(B) intrepidness...amalgamation
  brave...different
(D) inscrutability...remuneration
  secretive...rich
(E) vapidity...discord
  stupid...dislike

8. B (incontrovertible...ingenious)
  true...smart

(A) digressive...doltish
  irrelevant...stupid
(C) magnanimous...anomalous
  generous...different
(D) remunerative...mendacious
  rich...lying
(E) obsequious...pusillanimous
  to flatter...afraid

9. B (Scope: *Line 2*)
The word "dread" occurs in the context of memory loss. This negative connotation is best captured by the word "trepidation" or fear.

10. E (Scope: *Lines 8-10*)
The lines contain the phrase "it may actually", which implies something unexpected or surprising.

11. D (Scope: *Lines 20-33*)
In the passage, the long example of driving supports the author's claim about the key idea of the lines: semantic memory.

12. D (Scope: *Line 8*)
In the passage, the word "grave" is linked to a physical "condition". Only "serious" fits this context.

13. C (Scope: *Lines 35-38*)
Only this choice contains the lines' key ideas of "autobiographical memory" and "new stimuli".

14. C (Scope: *Paragraph 5*)
The key to this question lies in the concluding sentence of the paragraph (lines 53-54). In this context, "loss" (weakness) is actually a "gain" (strength).

15. A (Scope: *Line 51*)
In the passage, "precious" is linked with "mental resource". Only "invaluable", or beyond value, fits this context.

16. D (Scope: *Lines 55-58*)
The phrase "including me" (line 56) makes it clear that she counts herself as "an older person" (lines 55-56).

17. A (Scope: *Lines 15-19*)

Only choice (A) correctly captures the idea of the referenced lines by stating that explicit memory has two parts: autobiographical memory and semantic memory.

18. C (Scope: *Lines 35-38*)

Since children are always encountering new experiences, it follows that they rely heavily on autobiographical memory to process these experiences.

19. C (Scope: *Line 58*)

The word "strength" refers to the increasing reliance on semantic memory as a person ages. The benefits of such a situation are described in lines 49-53.

Section 2

1. D (hypothetical…obliterated)
    theoretical…destroy

(A) ambivalent…detracted
    unclear…take away
(B) profound…assuaged
    significant …make better
(C) colloquial…supplanted
    ordinary…replace
(E) illicit…delineated
    illegal…explain

2. A (a ravenous...rapacity)
    greedy…greedy

(B) a meager…liberality
    poor…generous
(C) a spurious…indigence
    false…poor
(D) an amorous…eccentricity
    passionate...odd
(E) an esoteric…listlessness
    strange…indifferent

3. D (debunk*: argue against*)

(A) concede: *give up*
(B) placate: *make better*
(C) dupe: *stupid*
(E) rectify: *make right*

4. E (bolster: *argue for*)

(A) concede: *give up*
(B) coax: *flatter*
(C) acknowledge: *admit*
(D) sanction: *approve*

5. D (conciliatory: *friendly*)

(A) flagrant: *obvious*
(B) precarious: *unsure*
(C) transient: *short-lived*
(E) misanthropic: *hate*

6. C (Scope: *Line 30*)
Within the context sentence, the idea is that genetically- engineered crops may be a "threat". Thus "hazard" most nearly means "danger".

7. A (Scope: *Passage 2*)
The author of Passage 2 does see the possibility of the advantages of the crops (line 34) but he also urges caution (lines 21-24). Only choice (A) captures these two attitudes.

8. E (Scope: *Passages 1 and 2*)
For the idea that modified crops may be "valuable", see lines 10-15 (Passage 1) and line 34 (Passage 2).

9. E (Scope: *Passages 1 and 2*)
Lines 15-18 contain a discussion about "apprehension", or fear, representing the sole obstacle towards improving lives. In order for the author of Passage 2 to respond effectively, he must address this "apprehension", potential reasons for which he gives in lines 24-31.

10. D (*Paragraph 1*)
The first paragraph focuses strictly on the historical facts of the rebellion, or insurrection.

11. B (*Lines 13-14*)
These lines turn from the history of the rebellion to the history of the leader of the rebellion, Nat Turner.

12. A (*Line 22*)
The context sentence is the culmination of the entire history of the man, Nat Turner. The fact that this history consists of only 3 or 4 brief facts supports the idea that the best definition for "paltry" is little or negligible.

13. E (*Whole Passage*)
In the passage, Gray is said to have "created the character of 'Nat Turner'" (lines 26-27). Choice (E) addresses this idea.

14. B (*Lines 34-37*)
These lines contain the ideas of "fears" and "the necessity to allay (calm) these fears". Only choice (B) addresses these ideas by referencing "alarm" and "its [alarm's] comfort".

15. E (Scope: *Line 41*)
In the passage, "the six novels" are said to "invent the details and motivations" of Nat Turner. This continues the idea that Nat Turner is an invented character.

16. C (Scope: *Lines 49-52*)
In the referenced lines, the author makes a calm and measured statement, an attitude best captured by "matter-of-fact".

17. E (Scope: *Paragraph 1*)
The first paragraph offers a concise history of the period immediately following the abolishment of the internment camps.

18. D (Scope: *Line 9*)
In paragraph 3, the author discusses the uncertainty of the living situations of returning Japanese-Americans. Only choice (D) fits this context.

19. B (Scope: *Line 14*)
The author quotes a man who discusses fear as his first or principal reason for not returning home. In context, the meaning of "chief" makes the best sense.

20. E (Scope: *Line 18*)
Since the man is quoted in the context of returning home, it can best be inferred that he means to bring his family home.

21. C (Scope: *Lines 17-20*)
These lines report knowledge of "resentment" among people in Los Angeles. This knowledge implies that news of discrimination against returning Japanese-Americans had reached the internment camps.

22. B (Scope: *Line 36-37*)
Since the passage discusses events that took place in the context of World War II (line 41), the best inference is that the lack of available workers is due to the war.

23. C (Scope: *Lines 46-48*)
The quoted man implies that he has been telling the story of internment for 50 years. His ongoing discussion of it and determination to keep telling it implies that the story has yet to fully comprehended.

24. E (Scope: *Line 33*)

In context the word "maintained" is contrasted with the sale of homes and businesses. Thus, the answer must be an antonym for "lose," and "kept" is the best answer.

Section 3

1. C (invalid...fallacious)
   false...false

(A) inscrutable…jaded
   secretive…indifferent
(B) conventional...craven
   widespread…afraid
(D) eccentric…laudatory
   odd…to praise
(E) penurious…rancorous
   poor…hate

2. D (unkempt: *messy*)

(A) bleak: *depressed*
(B) anomalous: *different*
(C) exhaustive: *thorough*
(E) flagrant: *obvious*

3. E (quixotic…dupe)
   different…stupid

(A) disparaging…commend
   insult…praise
(B) apathetic…rebuke
   indifferent…criticize
(C) eccentric…exalt
   different…praise
(D) tangential…abound
   irrelevant…a lot

4. E (discursive…pertinent)
   irrelevant…relevant

(A) amorous…aberrant
   passionate…different
(B) dubious…indubitable
   questioning…true
(C) impecunious…prodigal
   poor...rich
(D) arcane…commendable
   strange…to praise

5. C (contract: *make small*)

(A) bolster: *argue for*
(B) obscure: *unclear*
(D) affirm: *agree*
(E) diverge: *different*

6. D (expedient: *speed up*)

(A) cursory: *short-lived*
(B) implausible: *not possible*
(C) unwarranted: *undeserved*
(E) esoteric: *different / odd*

7. B (Scope: *Whole Passage*)

The passage describes Americans as "dependent" ("accepting") on cell phones even as many "despise" ("grudgingly") them.

8. E (Scope: *Whole Passage*)

Only choice (E) accurately captures the three key ideas in the passage: Americans, attitudes, and cell phones.

9. D (Scope: *Lines 17-18*)

Because Joel Engel is described as a "rival", the passage infers that Dr. Cooper phoned him because he enjoyed winning the competition to build the first cell phone.

10. C (Scope: *Whole Passage*)

Only choice (C) includes the main idea of the "invention" of the cell phone.

11. C (Scope: *Whole Passage*)

Only choice (C) captures the key idea of the need for a new system of organization for books, an idea that can be found throughout the entire passage.

12. A (Scope: *Whole Passage*)
On the one hand, the author praises the classification for those readers who know what they want (lines 3-7). On the other hand, the author wishes for a new system for those readers who do not know exactly what they want (lines 10-32). So "ambivalent", or unsure, is the best answer.

13. A (Scope: *Line 12*)
The best fit in context is "bold", a definition that the author uses to accentuate the problem of those who are uncertain as to what book they would like to read.

14. E (Scope: *Lines 27-30*)
These lines discuss "crammed" bookshelves and "interaction". This implication is summarized by choice (E).

15. B (Scope: *Line 34-38*)
In these lines, the author advocates immediate action, namely the rethinking of organization in libraries and bookstores. This idea of action is only found in choice (B).

16. D (Scope: *Lines 38-46*)
In these lines, the author suggests the arrangement of books by theme. This idea, the rearrangement of books by theme, primarily assume that books can be arranged by theme.

17. C (Scope: *Lines 11-15*)
The referenced lines accept the opinion given in lines 1-10and then continue on to enlarge the discussion of similarities between the architectural works.

18. C (Scope: *Lines 17-20*)
These lines undercut the "craziness" that might attend the outlandish theories in lines 11-15 by pointing out that they actually promote "prejudice" (line 20). These ideas are only found in choice (C).

19. E (Scope: *Line 32*)
The author continues her thesis of prejudice by using the example of the *conquistadors* and the Aymara. Only choice (E) contains these two groups of people.

20. C (Scope: *Line 39*)
The context tells us that the tourists flocked to see Tihuanaca, therefore they must have liked and been amazed by the city. Therefore, "praising" best fits the context of the passage.

21. D (Scope: *Line 37*)
The author obviously does not like racial prejudice, and she alludes to the prejudice of the "Europeans" in line 37. Therefore, her attitude is going to be critical.

22. D (Scope: *Line 41*)
Since the "old World" is brought up in the context of European travelers, it makes sense that it would be located in Europe. Of the answer choices, only Spain is in Europe.

23. D (Scope: *Line 53*)
The author makes a contrast between outsiders (giants, aliens, viracochas, etc.) who receive credit for native architecture and the natives themselves. Since she argues so strongly against the former group, she must believe that the ancestors of the original builders, the Amayra, should inherit Tihuanaca.

24. D (Scope: *Line 56*)
In the context sentence, the idea is that some modern theories are using extraterrestrial races.

SAT CRITICAL READING PRACTICE TEST 5

Time: 20 Minutes
19 Questions

Directions: Choose the answer that is grammatically correct, concise, and unambiguous.

1. Including only old-fashioned items such as Pilgrim hats, corsets, and doublets, Mary's wardrobe tends towards the -----.

(A) dogmatic   (B) listless   (C) lackadaisical
      (D) tentative   (E) antiquated

2. The mediator attempted to ----- the dispute by creating understanding between the parties; in the end, however, she could not quell their -----.

(A) exult…philanthropy
(B) debunk…implausibility
(C) mollify…contentiousness
(D) rebuke…conciliation
(E) palliate…inexorability

3. While the extremists' hateful speeches were tolerated by the citizens, they were not ----- by any of them.

(A) appeased   (B) condoned   (C) obscured
      (D) mollified   (E) bolstered

4. Jackson was disappointed by his ----- performance in the cheese-rolling competition, during which he had lacked energy and passion.

(A) lackadaisical (B) anomalous (C) flagrant
      (D) erroneous   (E) exhaustive

5. Despite numerous attempts to ----- the mistake, Frank was never able to fix the damage it caused.

(A) debunk   (B) rectify   (C) dupe
      (D) renounce   (E) sanction

6. An apology alone did not ----- Alan, who also demanded monetary damages in the aftermath of the accident.

(A) evade   (B) coax   (C) appease
      (D) concede   (E) rectify

7. The intricately-carved, ----- paneling, which covered the walls from floor to ceiling, added significantly to the party's ambience of -----.

(A) veracious…aversion
(B) munificent…trenchancy
(C) ornate…extravagance
(D) fatuous…stoutness
(E) overt…surreptitiousness

8. The super flu, more ----- than any previously-known strain, spread quickly and ----- until it affected all the continents.

(A) virulent…inexorably
(B) cerebral…perpetually
(C) craven…insuperably
(D) idiosyncratic…enigmatically
(E) robust…apprehensively

Questions 9-10 are based on the following passage.

According to most historians, the beginning of Egypt dates back to 3000 BCE, shortly before King Menes united Lower and Upper Egypt to form one nation. As a country
5 with a vast amount of history still to be uncovered, Egypt often appeals to archeologists as the perfect region for practical research. Over the centuries, many precious artifacts from Egypt have been lost. Others are
10 still waiting to be unearthed from the nation's terra firma. With so many opportunities for archeologists to attempt to fill in the puzzle pieces of Egypt's past, it often seems as though Egypt holds as many foreign visitors as it does
15 its own citizens.

9. In lines 4-8, the author primarily states that

(A) archeologists prefer to travel to Egypt
(B) Egypt is the oldest country and thus perfect for research
(C) archeologists conduct research in Egypt because of its partially unknown history
(D) ancient countries appeal to archeologists who wish to do research
(E) foreign visitors to Egypt are attempting to uncover the country's past

10. The primary purpose of the passage is to

(A) provoke resentment of foreigners among native Egyptians
(B) rebut the utility of scholarly research in Egypt
(C) engender enthusiasm among potential scholars of Egyptian history
(D) reiterate the necessity of research into Egypt's past
(E) highlight the magnitude of scholarly research in Egypt

Questions 11-12 are based on the following passage.

Ever since kindergarten, I was always one of the few students in my class with a drive to be as smart as I potentially could. Knowledge was my only hope of escaping the poor
5 conditions I lived under. While most of the other children in my neighborhood could have cared less about academic learning, I was never affected by their outward displays of apathy. Unfortunately, because both my parents were
10 always busy working to support us, they didn't paid much attention to my achievements at school. All that concerned them during my childhood was that I was doing exceptionally well on my report cards and I didn't need to be
15 monitored by anyone.

11. In lines 3-5, the author primarily states that

(A) few kindergarteners possess an eagerness to study
(B) education represents the sole means of advancement
(C) children who play cannot succeed in school
(D) his studying ensures his academic success
(E) friends distract from one's focus on studying

12. In lines 9-12, the author primarily states that his parents

(A) were generally not concerned with his well-being
(B) focused primarily on their own pursuits rather than their child's
(C) viewed school achievements with indifference
(D) remained preoccupied in an attempt to provide for the family
(E) regretted their limited involvement in their child's education

Questions 13-19 are based on the following passage.

Albert Einstein persists in the modern memory more than half a century beyond his death. According to one recent poll, while only 38% of Americans could name the serving
5 vice-president, 90% could identify Einstein. To this day, the phrase "You're no Einstein" carries currency. Indeed, there will only ever be one Einstein. Yet the Einstein of collective memory, the later Einstein, is perhaps not the
10 one that he himself would have chosen to be perpetuated.

This "political" Einstein was born in 1933, upon his immigration to Princeton, New Jersey. At this juncture he was already eighteen years
15 removed from his greatest scientific accomplishments: the proposal of the photoelectrical effect, the special theory of relativity, and the quantification in $E=mc^2$ of the relationship between mass and energy. He
20 was fifteen years into the quest to formulate a unified theory that integrated the gravitational and electromagnetic fields. This achievement, though he pursued it vigorously for more than three decades, would ultimately elude him.

25 In this span Einstein's primary role was a political one, as varying groups asked him to bear disparate causes. For his opinion held great sway with the public, which viewed him as a kind of citizen saint whose fierce
30 intelligence could be brought to bear on the important issues of the day. After an initial hesitance, Einstein publicly supported the establishment of Israel. He first advocated the creation of the atomic bomb during World War
35 II, and then disavowed it in favor of pacifism. He was one of the few figures who had the audacity to publicly dismiss and scorn the machinations of Joseph McCarthy and his search for "Un-American" activities.

40 In addition to considerable time, these involvements consumed intellectual effort. While Einstein never revealed the toll of these exertions to the public, his letters reveal it to be substantial. Indeed, only with generous thought
45 can a person shift his opinions on ponderous matters as Einstein did. Yet one must continue to wonder about the ultimate cost of Einstein's political efforts to his science.

13. Lines 3-5 primarily serve to

(A) punctuate the pervasive renown of Einstein
(B) scoff at the ignorance of Americans
(C) advocate the depiction of Einstein on currency
(D) invalidate the widespread obscurity of Einstein
(E) laud the utility of polls that survey the public

14. In line 7, the word "currency" most nearly means

(A) money
(B) current
(C) general use
(D) cash
(E) prevalence

15. Lines 12-16 primarily serve to

(A) tout the process by which Einstein accomplished his scientific feats
(B) reinforce the distinction between Einstein's early life and his later life
(C) underscore the scientific failures that proceeded the listed achievements
(D) delineate the significance of the photoelectrical effect to science
(E) justify Einstein's later fame

16. In line 44, the word "generous" most nearly means

(A) unselfish
(B) kind
(C) munificent
(D) large
(E) plentiful

17. Lines 31-39 serve primarily to

(A) complement Einstein's scientific attainments
(B) proffer instances of Einstein's political activities
(C) hail Einstein's conversion to pacifism
(D) censure the political actions of McCarthy
(E) defend Einstein's political involvements

18. The main idea of the passage is

(A) the enduring legacy of Einstein and his scientific
     achievements
(B) Einstein's life and career in America
(C) the manner in which Einstein's science informed
     his politics
(D) the division in Einstein's life between the
     scientific and the political
(E) the catalysts for Einstein's political engagement

19. Lines 46-48 primarily imply that
(A) Einstein's political efforts were ill-served by his
     science
(B) scientists should not involve themselves in the
     political arena
(C) Einstein ultimately broke under the weight of his
     political obligations
(D) Einstein's politics were disparaged by his
     contemporaries
(E) Einstein's scientific efforts suffered because of
     his political ones

END SECTION

Time: 25 Minutes
24 Questions

Directions: Choose the answer that is grammatically correct, concise, and unambiguous.

---

1. The somberness he believed would be ----- turned out to be a merely ----- sadness that passed in a few days.

(A) ephemeral…abstruse
(B) perpetual…evanescent
(C) fawning…adulatory
(D) salient…trenchant
(E) eternal…obscure

2. Skeptics suspected the ----- of the report when its author made explicit, ----- references to groups that were indubitably fabrications and frauds.

(A) profusion…altruistic
(B) inscrutability…audacious
(C) legitimacy…overt
(D) mendacity…surreptitious
(E) élan…coaxing

3. Although at first glance their ideas appeared quite -----, closer inspection revealed them to be very similar.

(A) antiquated   (B) erroneous   (C) divergent
    (D) listless   (E) transient

4. Critics dismissed the event as an obvious, ----- attempt to gain influence and political power.

(A) flagrant   (B) evasive   (C) cursory
    (D) bleak   (E) esoteric

5. Many French filmmakers of the 1960s considered themselves -----, breaking cinematic ground and forever eclipsing other techniques and narratives that they considered to be trite.

(A) befuddled   (B) fugacious   (C) imperishable
    (D) profligate   (E) avant-garde

Questions 6-16 are based on the following passage.
The passage comes from a 19ᵗʰ-century novel.

I did not faint, but the effort to realize my
position made me very giddy, and I remember
that my companion had to give me a strong
arm as he conducted me from the roof to a
5 roomy apartment on the upper floor of the
house, where he insisted on my drinking a
glass or two of good wine and partaking of a
light repast.

"I think you are going to be all right now,"
10 he said cheerily. "I should not have taken so
abrupt a means to convince you of your
position if your course, while perfectly
excusable under the circumstances, had not
rather obliged me to do so. I confess," he added
15 laughing, "I was a little apprehensive at one
time that I should undergo what I believe you
used to call a knockdown in the nineteenth
century, if I did not act rather promptly. I
remembered that the Bostonians of your day
20 were famous pugilists, and thought best to lose
no time. I take it you are now ready to acquit
me of the charge of hoaxing you."

"If you had told me," I replied, profoundly
awed, "that a thousand years instead of a
25 hundred had elapsed since I last looked on this
city, I should now believe you."

"Only a century has passed," he answered,
"but many a millennium in the world's history
has seen changes less extraordinary."

30 "And now," he added, extending his hand
with an air of irresistible cordiality, "let me
give you a hearty welcome to the Boston of the
twentieth century and to this house. My name
is Leete, Dr. Leete they call me."

35 "My name," I said as I shook his hand, "is
Julian West."

"I am most happy in making your
acquaintance, Mr. West," he responded.
"Seeing that this house is built on the site of
40 your own, I hope you will find it easy to make
yourself at home in it."

After my refreshment Dr. Leete offered me
a bath and a change of clothing, of which I
gladly availed myself.

45 It did not appear that any very startling
revolution in men's attire had been among the
great changes my host had spoken of, for,
barring a few details, my new habiliments did
not puzzle me at all.

50 Physically, I was now myself again. But
mentally, how was it with me, the reader will
doubtless wonder. What were my intellectual
sensations, he may wish to know, on finding
myself so suddenly dropped as it were into a
55 new world? In reply let me ask him to suppose
himself suddenly, in the twinkling of an eye,
transported from earth, say, to Paradise or
Hades. What does he fancy would be his own
experience? Would his thoughts return at once
60 to the earth he had just left, or would he, after
the first shock, wellnigh forget his former life
for a while, albeit to be remembered later, in
the interest excited by his new surroundings?

All I can say is, that if his experience were
65 at all like mine in the transition I am
describing, the latter hypothesis would prove
the correct one. The impressions of amazement
and curiosity which my new surroundings
produced occupied my mind, after the first
70 shock, to the exclusion of all other thoughts.

For the time the memory of my former life
was, as it were, in abeyance. No sooner did I
find myself physically rehabilitated through the
kind offices of my host, than I became eager to
75 return to the house-top; and presently we were
comfortably established there in easy-chairs,
with the city beneath and around us. After Dr.
Leete had responded to numerous questions on
my part, as to the ancient landmarks I missed
80 and the new ones which had replaced them, he
asked me what point of the contrast between
the new and the old city struck me most
forcibly.

6. Lines 4-8 primarily suggest that

(A) West is suffering from a grave illness
(B) Dr. Leete is physically powerful
(C) the city poses a danger to the companions
(D) Dr. Leete is a generous host
(E) West is intoxicated by his new surroundings

7. Lines 15-18 primarily indicate that

(A) Dr. Leete had feared violence from West
(B) West had been a renowned boxer in his era
(C) Boston had been the home of the best pugilists
(D) West had knocked Dr. Leete down once before
(E) Dr. Leete had been an avid fan of boxing

8. In line 12, the word "course" most nearly means

(A) duration
(B) succession
(C) area
(D) class
(E) action

9. According to the passage, West is from which of the following centuries?

(A) 9th century
(B) 10th century
(C) 19th century
(D) 20th century
(E) 21st century

10. Lines 39-41 primarily suggest that

(A) West is uncomfortable in his new surroundings
(B) Dr. Leete is playing a trick on West
(C) West and Dr. Leete are roommates
(D) Dr. Leete is selling his home to West
(E) Dr. Leete and West share a common geography

11. In lines 52-55, the author primarily employs which of the following devices

(A) irony
(B) allusion
(C) rhetorical questioning
(D) hyperbole
(E) personification

12. In line 58, the word "fancy" most nearly means

(A) visualize
(B) fine
(C) imagine
(D) decorate
(E) love

13. In lines 71-72, the author primarily suggests that West

(A) enjoys proving abstruse hypotheses correct
(B) and Dr. Leete share the same experience
(C) cannot remember his prior experiences
(D) and Dr. Leete are interested in the city
(E) remains in a state of astonished shock

14. In line 74, the word "offices" most nearly means

(A) beneficial acts
(B) formal duties
(C) authoritative positions
(D) governmental departments
(E) public positions

15. According to the passage, West's attitude towards the "ancient landmarks" (line 79) is one of

(A) ironic detachment
(B) wistful longing
(C) utter awe
(D) mild affection
(E) hardened rancor

16. By the end of the passage, the relationship between West and Dr. Leete can best be identified as one between two

(A) antagonists
(B) sycophants
(C) sages
(D) acquaintances
(E) cynics

Questions 17-24 are based on the following passage.

The manners of communication are surprisingly pervasive and enduring. The rules for the most elevated form of verbal communication, conversation, have been
5   codified in manuals for at least 2,000 years. Its basic principles seem to be nearly universal, covering such ideas as the rudeness of interruption and the inadvisability of incessantly talking about yourself.
10   Only in recent times, however, has the attempt been made to understand the intricacies of non-verbal communication, which can impart far more meaning than any word. Every conscious minute, people are communicating
15   through seemingly simple and inconsequential acts. Raising an eyebrow or making a fist signals unspoken disagreement. Lowering an eyebrow or shrugging a shoulder indicates submission, even while the most defiant words
20   are spoken. These gestures are nearly universal in their meaning, and a purer form of communication than verbal conversation.
        Let's take the story of Wesley and Jane, college acquaintances who happen to meet at a
25   coffee shop several years after graduation. Upon meeting Jane, Wesley begins to blink rapidly as he explains that he is now a lawyer currently working in a large firm. Jane makes a fist beneath a table, as she mentions that she
30   has done work with the same firm. Wesley then looks down at his watch, apologizing to Jane because he is late for a meeting and assuring her that it was nice to see her again. Before he leaves, however, Wesley says that they should
35   get together again soon and passes her his phone number. Crossing her arms before her chest, Jane agrees wholeheartedly and promises to call Wesley soon.
        The question now is whether Jane will call
40   Wesley. If verbal communication was the sole guide, the answer would have to be in the affirmative. The reality is otherwise. For Wesley is not really a lawyer. Rapid blinking signals that he is lying about his profession, a
45   fact that Jane understands and reacts to by clenching her fist. From that point forward, Jane's non-verbal communication signals opposition. While her words signal that she would love to see him again, her crossed arms

50   convey a truer and more profound meaning.
        While an analysis of this story can now be achieved with current knowledge, further rigorous study is necessary for a fuller understanding of the means and messages of
55   non-verbal communication. Specifically, the physiological processes that lead to movements, such as eye blinking or fist clenching, require deeper understanding. Otherwise, we all will continue to proffer most
60   communication without knowledge of the what, the how, or the why.

17. The primary purpose of the first paragraph is to

(A) vindicate an unpopular point of view
(B) propose an inherent link between verbal and non-verbal communication
(C) illustrate the difficulties of conversation
(D) provide a contrast to a disparate form of communication
(E) rebut the rules employed by good conversationalists

18. In line 2, the word "enduring" most nearly means

(A) brave
(B) persistent
(C) suffering
(D) tolerant
(E) supportive

19. In lines 10-13, the author argues that

(A) the most meaningful communication is conveyed through the simplest acts
(B) verbal communication represents a complex undertaking
(C) the comprehension of non-verbal communication is still in an early phase
(D) non-verbal communication has lasted longer than verbal communication
(E) all communication has either explicit or implicit rules which people must follow

20. Lines 16-20 can best be described as

(A) a rebuke of the rules of non-verbal communication
(B) an endorsement of verbal communication
(C) a demystification of all the non-verbal signals of submission
(D) a series of examples of non-verbal communication and their respective meanings
(E) an account of the opposing meanings of verbal and non-verbal communication

21. By using the phrase "purer form" (line 21), the author primarily indicates that

(A) verbal communication is more uniform than non-verbal communication
(B) non-verbal communication is more theoretical than verbal communication
(C) verbal communication is more complete than non-verbal communication
(D) non-verbal communication is more direct than verbal communication
(E) communication is cleaner than no communication

22. Based on the passage, the story of Wesley and Jane in the 3rd paragraph most likely represents

(A) a hypothetical story about the pervasiveness of lying
(B) a common narrative of betrayed friendship
(C) a personal anecdote offered as an example
(D) a fictional work presented for analysis
(E) an excerpt from a much larger work on honesty

23. Based on the passage, which of the following most likely represents the "what" (line 61)?

(A) basic physiology
(B) unconscious acts
(C) universal rules
(D) recognized motivations
(E) transmitted significance

24. Lines 51-55 can best be described as

(A) a reassessment of a previous theory
(B) a call for future action
(C) a pithy anecdote
(D) a validation of non-verbal communication
(E) a critique of scientists

END SECTION

Time: 25 Minutes
24 Questions

Directions: Choose the answer that is grammatically correct, concise, and unambiguous.

---

1. The beauty's suitors contrived ----- means to ----- the woman they loved, showering her with a wealth of songs, poems, and dedications.

(A) munificent...affront
(B) stingy...adulate
(C) erudite...abominate
(D) insipid...reprimand
(E) profuse...laud

2. Her deep, growling voice struck some people as being ----- with her short, petite frame.

(A) gratuitous   (B) feasible   (C) comprehensive
     (D) impossible   (E) incongruous

3. He remembered that when he was a child the -----, clear waters of the stream had supported a profusion of fish; now, just two decades later, the same waters were so ----- that he could not see any fish, even if he could see to its bottom.

(A) idle...malignant
(B) limpid...turbid
(C) nonplussed...opaque
(D) potent...jejune
(E) quotidian...deferential

4. Although he could fabricate and ----- with great facility, the ---- and copious number of his lies guaranteed that, one day, he would not be able to keep them straight and his falsehoods would be manifest.

(A) squander...evaluative
(B) dupe...avid
(C) besmirch...befuddled
(D) bootlick...malleable
(E) dissemble...prodigious

5. The best teachers utilize concrete examples to illustrate ----- ideas and theories.

(A) contentious   (B) incongruous   (C) peripheral
     (D) abstract   (E) prudent

6. Sharing the ----- of her parents, the child deeply feared black mirrors and broken cats.

(A) adulation   (B) embellishment (C) apprehension (D)
     decorum   (E) prey

Questions 7-8 are based on the following passage.

Rather, it is a failure of critics and of criticism itself, which is happily ignored by gamers. Criticism has evolved very smartly to handle the narrative. A poem can be dissected
5   and significance extracted from its smallest organ. A novel can be squeezed by different scholars to conform to ideas that seem mutually exclusive. Movies are endlessly scoured for the "why", and scorned if they lack
10 sense.

While these art forms remain static, however, a video game mutates each and every time it is played. A game can be experienced by millions of players simultaneously; yet,
15 each player will derive a disparate meaning from the event. In this new frontier, it no longer makes sense to ask what a video game signifies. Instead, video games must be scoured for their potentiality of implication. In
20 other words, the starting point of any truly critical understanding of video games must begin with one question: "What could they mean?"

7. The primary purpose of the passage is to

(A) clarify the meaning of video games
(B) vindicate the interests of video gamers
(C) advocate a critical approach to video games
(D) denounce the video game industry
(E) elucidate the revelations of video gamers

8. Lines 11-13 draw a primary distinction between

(A) the dynamism of video games and the fixed nature of other art forms
(B) the shared experience of video games and the solitary experience of other art forms
(C) the opinions of video gamers and those of critics
(D) the sense of movies and that of other art forms
(E) the significance of video games and that of art forms such as the novel

Questions 9-10 are based on the following passage.

Another important issue with the marker of literary minimalism is that the distinctions between wordy and simplified writing styles aren't as easy to differentiate as subject, era,
5   culture and region. What appears to some readers and critics as modest in terms of vocabulary can often appear to others as quite complicated in terms of grammar, and vice versa: especially when the two pieces being
10 compared are written in different languages. In some cases readers deem authors' works minimalist, even when the authors themselves believe their works fit into other genres.

9. In lines 4-5, "subject, era, culture and region" are examples of

(A) topics addressed by literary minimalists
(B) ideas integral to the success of minimalist authors
(C) genres employed in minimalist literature
(D) plot devices avoided by minimalist writers
(E) criteria utilized to classify literature

10. In line 6, the word "modest" most nearly means

(A) humble
(B) small
(C) lowly
(D) inferior
(E) simple

Questions 11-17 are based on the following passage.

The elderly gentleman looked kind enough
as he accounted for the origin of the carving.
He explained that it had been passed down to
him by his grandfather, who had worked in
5   Alaska sometime during the 19th century. The
appraiser nodded and I tuned out her excited
prattle, wondering why I was filled with such
sudden rage.

I focused on the carving for answers. It
10 was diminutive, smaller than my palm, and
made from walrus tusk. Upon closer reflection,
the masterfulness of the animal's execution
was apparent in the delicate curves of its paws
and jaw line. Yet the bear, a vital figure in Inuit
15 culture, still exuded a majestic power in the
subtle muscling of its torso and legs.

The source of my fury, I then
apprehended, lay not in the carving but in the
appraiser. Her smooth discussion of lineage
20 and auction value belied a fundamental
injustice. She could not assess the worth of
such a piece, removed as she was from the
carving in time and in customs. Her assessment
of four thousand dollars represented a slight, an
25 affront to the Inuit who crafted the piece and to
his culture.

No, it was the old man who was at fault.
His blithe unknowingness of the carving's
history disgusted me. His benign smile
30 masked, I was now certain, a pedestrian greed.
His connection to the carving ran no deeper
than the dollars it would fetch. Having reached
the limits of pique, I snapped the television off.

Months passed before the ancient bear
35 charged back into my heart. It thundered and
roared, before stooping down to gnaw upon my
wrath. The appraiser had merely been doing
her job, valuing the past. The elderly man had
clearly cherished the carving as a link in his
40 chain of personal history. His grandfather had
probably not stolen the carving from an
ancestor, contrary to my prior imaginings of
underhanded thievery.

Suddenly the bear fled, and with it fury,
45 leaving behind only the tender grief to mourn
what could never be recovered or redeemed.

11. Lines 21-23 indicate that the obstacles that the appraiser faces are primarily

(A) cultural and chronological
(B) sociological and aesthetic
(C) emotional and intellectual
(D) financial and monetary
(E) artistic and creative

12. In line 24, the word "slight" most nearly means

(A) meagerness
(B) worthlessness
(C) insult
(D) weakness
(E) unimportance

13. According to lines 29-32, the author believes that the old man primarily views the carving as

(A) an unimportant trifle
(B) a stunning work of craftsmanship
(C) a valuable memento of family history
(D) a potent symbol of Inuit culture
(E) a precious commodity

14. In line 32, the word "fetch" most nearly means

(A) carry
(B) obtain
(C) take
(D) bear
(E) retrieve

15. Lines 37-43 primarily represent

(A) a rebuff of the old man and the appraiser
(B) a clarification of previously stated opinions
(C) an apology to the old man and the appraiser
(D) a criticism of appraisers and auctions
(E) a reassessment of prior speculations

16. The last paragraph primarily indicates that the author

(A) has completely forgotten about the carving
(B) has reached a state of dispassion
(C) has come to uncertain terms with the old man's
        possession of the carving
(D) has maintained his anger at the injustice of the
        situation
(E) has forever lost contact with the bear carving

17. Which of the following is implied in the passage?

(A) The bear carving was stolen from an Inuit.
(B) The author has bought the bear carving.
(C) The value of the bear carving has steadily
        increased over time.
(D) The bear is the central figure in Inuit culture.
(E) The author is descended from the Inuit.

Questions 18-24 are based on the following passage.

The fact that many of the social problems among inner city youth come from a lack of proper education is no surprise to New York City educators. However, the best solution is
5   still a source of debate among parents and educators. Lee Cohen, a long-time public school teacher in the South Bronx, has recently begun working for an alternative public school called The Bronx Guild, which focuses a
10   significant amount of individual attention on each student in an attempt to ascertain their personal interests. The purpose of this style of teaching is to then use that awareness to find specific areas of education that might serve a
15   practical purpose to them in the future.

     Cohen explains to parents that if a student is interested in becoming a studio engineer, the school's faculty then make sure he or she receive access to all of the school's music
20   classes. Similarly, if a student is interested in one day becoming a business employee, they assign him or her specific paper topics focused on America's business world. According to Cohen, in some cases students come back to
25   class the next week with even more of a desire to pursue those fields, which the faculty immediately take note of. Other times students come back saying, "I'm no longer interested in that".

30   While schools like The Bronx Guild are still quite rare within the five boroughs of New York City, many educational workers with a concern for inner city youth are beginning to hail their advantages. One of the head faculty
35   members at The Guild, Joan Johanson, explains that educators and parents should be realistic in accepting that not every student will be able to, nor care to, immediately apply to college after high school. Therefore, the faculty
40   does their best to prepare them for internships in fields that they find interesting once they graduate.

     On the other hand, there are those who believe specialized schools like The Bronx
45   Guild bring more harm than good to adolescents over the long run. With an equal degree of concern for each student's welfare, skeptical educators and parents contend that alternative educations limit the potential

50   achievements of teenagers and children. Just as Cohen and Johanson see individualized attention as the key, many educators argue that every student should be learning Math, Science, History, English and Physical
55   Education throughout high school. If not, then perhaps parents will never know how far their children might have succeeded in all traditional scholastic areas.

     Johanson acknowledges that it is not
60   always easy to exploit every student's personal educational interests, and sometimes students do miss out on other opportunities when they're guided in the wrong direction. However, her view remains that as long as
65   schools like The Bronx Guild do their best to put students where they potentially belong, less youth will be on the streets after 12th grade.

18. The main idea of the passage is that

(A) oppositionists may eventually come to terms with alternative forms of education
(B) educators understand the future of inner-city children better than their parents
(C) all students in the inner city should have access to traditional core subjects
(D) no workable solution for educating inner city youth will likely be reached
(E) alternative education remains a source of disagreement among parents and educators

19. In lines 12-20, the attitude of teachers at Bronx Guild towards their students' educational pursuits can best be described as one of

(A) open hostility
(B) flexible pragmatism
(C) solemn respect
(D) unqualified approval
(E) frustrated resignation

20. In the second paragraph, an underlying assumption of the Bronx Guild school is that

(A) students should never take core subjects such as Math and English
(B) the school has classes or assignments to match every student's interests
(C) alternative education helps students better express their interests
(D) the school's classes are superior to those of schools with traditional curricula
(E) most students are interested in pursuing careers in music or business

21. The attitude of "educators and parents" (line 36) towards alternative education can best be described as one of

(A) condescension
(B) nostalgia
(C) approval
(D) derision
(E) cynicism

22. The "educators" in line 27 assume that
(A) parents want their children to study traditional scholastic subjects
(B) the majority of students in alternative schools will not choose to study traditional subjects
(C) Math is essential to the future career success of all children
(D) the Bronx Guild unintentionally hurts their student's future success
(E) Johanson is misguided in her educational philosophies

23. In the passage, the tone of the author can best be described as

(A) genuinely perplexed
(B) unabashedly admiring
(C) openly disdainful
(D) respectfully objective
(E) grudgingly empathetic

24. The author's organizes the passage by

(A) offering an opinion, presenting examples, and making a conclusion
(B) presenting a dilemma, examining a possible solution, and probing a contrary proposal
(C) recounting a story, exploring its characters, and drawing a conclusion
(D) stating a thesis, offering supporting examples, and rebutting counterarguments
(E) stating a problem, examining its history, and summarizing its impact

END SECTION

Practice Test 5
Answer Key and Explanations

Section 1

1. E
2. C
3. B
4. A
5. B
6. C
7. C
8. A
9. C
10. E
11. B
12. D
13. A
14. C
15. B
16. E
17. B
18. D
19. E

Section 2

1. B
2. C
3. C
4. A
5. E
6. D
7. A
8. E
9. C
10. E
11. C
12. C
13. C
14. A

15. B
16. D
17. D
18. B
19. C
20. D
21. D
22. D
23. E
24. B

Section 3

1. E
2. E
3. B
4. E
5. D
6. C
7. C
8. A
9. E
10. E
11. A
12. C
13. E
14. B
15. E
16. C
17. E
18. E
19. B
20. B
21. E
22. C
23. D
24. B

Finding Your Score

Raw score: Total Number Right – [Total Number Wrong ÷ 4] = _____

Notes: 1) Omissions are not counted towards your raw score
        2) If the total number wrong ÷ 4 ends in .5 or .75, it is rounded up

Critical Reading Scoring Table			
Raw Score	Scaled Score	Raw Score	Scaled Score
67	800	32	540
66	800	31	530
65	800	30	520
64	800	29	520
63	780	28	510
62	770	27	500
61	760	26	500
60	740	25	490
59	730	24	480
58	720	23	470
57	710	22	460
56	700	21	460
55	690	20	450
54	680	19	440
53	670	18	430
52	660	17	430
51	660	16	420
50	650	15	420
49	640	14	400
48	630	13	390
47	630	12	380
46	620	11	370
45	610	10	370
44	610	9	360
43	600	8	350
42	590	7	340
41	590	6	330
40	580	5	320
39	580	4	310
38	570	3	300
37	560	2	280
36	560	1	260
35	550	0	240
34	550	-1	220
33	540	-2	200

Identifying Strengths and Areas for Improvement

Go back to the test and circle the questions that you answered incorrectly. This review will allow you to see what answer explanations to study more closely for problem-solving techniques. It will also allow you to see what question types and passage types you need to review more carefully.

	Section 1	Section 2	Section 3
Passage Types			
Aesthetics / Arts			7-8
Biography	13-19		
Fiction		6-16	11-17
History			
Hard Sciences		17-24	
Social Sciences			9-10, 18-24
Question Types			
Assumption			20, 22
Attitude / Tone		15	19, 21, 23
Inference	19	6, 7, 10, 13, 16, 21, 22, 23	16, 17
Literal Comprehension	9, 11, 12, 13, 15, 17	9, 19	8, 9, 11, 13
Main Idea	18		18
Primary Purpose	10	17	7
Structure		11, 20, 24	15, 24
Word-in-Context	14, 16	8, 12, 14, 18	10, 12, 14

Section 1

1. E (antiquated: *old*)

(A) dogmatic: *stubborn*
(B) listless: *lazy / indifferent*
(C) lackadaisical: *lazy / indifferent*
(D) tentative: *unsure*

2. C (mollify…contentiousness)
  make better…unfriendly
(A) exult…philanthropy
  praise…generous
(B) debunk…implausibility
  argue against…impossible
(D) rebuke…conciliation
  argue against…friendly
(E) palliate…inexorability
  make better …stubborn

3. B (condoned: *approve*)

(A) appeased: *make better*
(C) obscured: *unclear*
(D) mollified: *make better*
(E) bolstered: *argue for*

4. A (lackadaisical: *lazy / indifferent*)

(B) anomalous: *different*
(C) flagrant: *obvious*
(D) erroneous: *error*
(E) exhaustive: *thorough*

5. B (rectify: *make right*)

(A) debunk: *argue against*
(C) dupe: *stupid*
(D) renounce: *reject*
(E) sanction: *approve*

6. C (appease: *make better*)

(A) evade: *avoid*
(B) coax: *flatter*
(D) concede: *give up*
(E) rectify: *make right*

7. C (ornate...extravagance)
  rich…rich

(A) veracious…aversion
  true…dislike
(B) munificent…trenchancy
  generous…relevant
(D) fatuous…stoutness
  stupid...brave
(E) overt…surreptitiousness
  obvious…secretive

8. A (virulent…inexorably)
  harmful…strong

(B) cerebral…perpetually
  smart…long-lived
(C) craven…insuperably
  afraid…strong
(D) idiosyncratic…enigmatically
  different…secret
(E) robust…apprehensively
  strong…afraid

9. C (Scope: *Lines 4-8*)

Only choice (C) contains the key ideas in the referenced lines: archaeologists, research, and Egypt.

10. E (Scope: *Whole Passage*)

Choice (E) contains the main ideas of the entire passage: scholars, research, and Egypt.

11. B (Scope: *Lines 3-5*)

In the referenced lines, the author states that knowledge ("education") was the one and only ("sole") way to escape ("advancement").

12. D (Scope: *Lines 9-12*)

The referenced lines state that the author's parents were busy ("preoccupied") supporting ("providing for") the family.

13. A (Scope: *Lines 3-5*)
The referenced lines highlight Einstein's continuing fame and recognition, an idea that only choice (A) addresses.

14. C (Scope: *Line 7*)
The context sentence implies that the statement is still used by people. Only "general use" holds this idea.

15. B (Scope: *Lines 12-16*)
Within these lines, the author emphasizes the beginning of the "political Einstein", differentiating him by distancing him from the earlier scientific feats of "scientific" Einstein.

16. E (Scope: *Line 44*)
In context, the author reveals that the answer must be a synonym for "substantial" (line 39). Only "plentiful" in choice (E) fits this context.

17. B (Scope: *Lines 31-39*)
These lines contain multiple examples of Einstein's political involvements.

18. D (Scope: *Whole Passage*)
The key idea of the passage is "Einstein" and the division between his earlier "scientific" life and his later "political life". Only choice (D) correctly includes these elements.

19. E (Scope: *Lines 46-48*)
These lines contain both the idea of "science" and of "politics". Only choice (E) captures these ideas in the sense conveyed by the author in the passage.

Section 2

(E) B (perpetual…evanescent)
   long-lived…short-lived

(E) ephemeral…abstruse
   short-lived…secret
(E) ©fawning…adulatory
   flatter…flatter
(D) salient…trenchant
   obvious…relevant
(E) eternal…obscure
   long-lived…unclear

2. C (legitimacy…overt)
   true…obvious

(A) profusion…altruistic
   rich…generous
(B) inscrutability…audacious
   secretive…brave
(D) mendacity…surreptitious
   lying…secretive
(E) élan…coaxing
   passionate…to flatter

3. C (divergent: *different*)

(A) antiquated: *old*
(B) erroneous: *error*
(D) listless: *lazy / indifferent*
(E) transient: *short-lived*

4. A (flagrant: *obvious*)

(B) evasive: *avoid*
(C) cursory: *short-lived*
(D) bleak: *depressed*
(E) esoteric: *different / odd*

5. E (avant-garde: *original*)
(A) befuddled: *confused*
(B) fugacious: *short-lived*
(C) imperishable: *long-lived*
(D) profligate: *using a lot*

6. D (Scope: *Lines 4-8*)
The referenced lines depict Dr. Leete helping West into the apartment and offering him food and drink. These actions indicate that Dr. Leete is a generous host.

7. A (Scope: *Lines 15-18*)
The lines indicate that Leete was "apprehensive...about a knockdown". Only Choice (A) addresses this idea.

8. E (Scope: *Line 12*)
In the context sentence, Leete explains his past actions by referencing West's own "course", or actions.

9. C (Scope: *Whole Passage*)
In lines 15-16, Leete indicates that West is from the 19th century by trying to use 19th-century terms. Additionally, lines 21-31 state that West has slept for 100 years and that Leete welcomes West to the 20th century.

10. E (Scope: *Lines 39-41*)
These lines indicate that West and Leete have lived in the same place.

11. C (Scope: *Lines 52-55*)
The lines consist of a question that the narrator (West) does not expect an answer to. This is a rhetorical question.

12. C (Scope: *Line 58*)
The context sentence invites the reader to "fancy" himself in exactly the same situation as the narrator. The best definition for this context is "imagine".

13. C (Scope: *Lines 71-72*)
The "exclusion of all other thoughts" includes the forgetting of all past experiences on the part of West.

14. A (Scope: *Line 74*)
The context sentence includes the idea of kindness ("kind"), which suggests that the "offices" are beneficial.

15. B (Scope: *Line 79*)
These lines indicate that the shock of "missed" landmarks provokes a response from West. Since the buildings he had known earlier have been replaced by new buildings, the best indication is that West longs for familiar landmarks.

16. D (Scope: *Whole Passage*)
This question relies primarily upon vocabulary knowledge. Since West and Leete have gotten to know each other a bit within the passage, the only appropriate fit is "acquaintances".

17. D (Scope: *First Paragraph*)
The first paragraph discusses only verbal communication, thereby setting up a contrast for the topic of the rest of the passage, non-verbal communication.

18. B (Scope: *Line 2*)
The context of the passage imparts the idea of lasting a long time, "at least 2,000 years" (line 5). Therefore, the best definition for "enduring" is "persisting", or long-lived.

19. C (Scope: *Lines 10-13*)
The ideas presented in these lines include "recent times" and "understanding". These ideas are reflected in the answer choice: "early phase" and "comprehension".

20. D (Scope: *Lines 16-20*)
These lines list a series of examples of non-verbal communication ("raising an eyebrow") and then explicate the respective meanings of these actions ("disagreement").

21. D (Scope: *Line 21*)
In the context of the passage, the author's description of non-verbal communication as "pure" immediately follows a description of how words can lie and distort meaning (lines 17-18). This contrast supports the idea that non-verbal communication is more direct than verbal communication.

22. D (Scope: *Paragraph 3*)
The key idea is analysis. After relating the story in the paragraphs, the author then analyzes the story in the 4th paragraph.

23. E (Scope: *Line 61 and Whole Passage*)
In lines 46-49, the author makes specific mention of the need to better understand "the means and messages" of nonverbal communication. The means correspond to the "why" (line 54), while the "what" (line 54) corresponds to the messages.

24. B (Scope: *Lines 51-55*)

In these lines the author advocates "further rigorous study," a phenomenon that would demand future action.

Section 3

1. E (profuse...laud)
    rich...to praise

(A) munificent...affront
    generous...to insult
(B) stingy...adulate
    greedy...to flatter
(C) erudite...abominate
    smart...hate
(D) insipid...reprimand
    stupid...to scold

2. E (incongruous: *indifferent*)

(A) gratuitous: *unnecessary*
(B) feasible: *possible*
(C) comprehensive: *thorough*
(D) impossible: *not possible*

3. B (limpid...turbid)
    clear...unclear

(A) idle...malignant
    lazy...harmful
(C) nonplussed...opaque
    confused...unclear
(D) potent...jejune
    strong...boring
(E) quotidian...deferential
    ordinary...obedient

4. E (dissemble...prodigious)
    false / lying...large

(A) squander...evaluative
    using a lot...questioning
(B) dupe...avid
    stupid...passionate
(C) besmirch...befuddled
    insult...confused
(D) bootlick...malleable
    flatter...obedient

5. D (abstract: *theoretical*)

(A) contentious: *unfriendly*
(B) incongruous: *different*
(C) peripheral: *irrelevant*
(E) prudent: *cautious*

6. C (apprehension: *afraid*)

(A) adulation: *flatter*
(B) embellishment: *decorate*
(D) decorum: *polite*
(E) prey: *hunted*

7. C (Scope: *Whole Passage*)
The key ideas throughout the passage are "criticism" and "video games". The "critical approach" is in lines 19-23.

8. A (Scope: *Lines 11-13*)
The distinction made is between the "static" (line 25) and constantly "mutat[ing]" (line 26) or changing.

9. E (Scope: *Whole Passage*)
In the passage the words "differentiate" (line 4) and "genres" (line 10) indicate the author's discussion of classification. The idea of literature can be inferred from the author's mention of "writing styles" (line 3) and "authors" (line 12).

10. E (Scope: *Line 6*)
In context, the word "modest" is contrasted with "complicated" (line 8). Thus "simple" is the best definition.

11. A (Scope: *Lines 21-23*)
These lines reference both "time" and "culture". These match "chronological" and "cultural" in choice (A).

12. C (Scope: *Line 24*)
The context sentence betrays a sense of injustice, which the author conveys using the word "affront", or insult.

13. E (Scope: *Lines 29-32*)
In the lines, the author mentions the man's "greed" and concern with "dollars", implying that the man views the carving as a commodity, or object to be sold.

14. B (Scope: *Line 32*)
The context sentence mentions the "dollars it would fetch", providing the sense of "getting", or "obtaining".

15. E (Scope: *Lines 37-43*)
In these lines, the author systematically revises opinions stated in lines 16-31. This revision is a "reassessment".

16. C (Scope: *6th Paragraph*)
This paragraph states that, while the author's rage has subsided, it has been replaced with a lasting sadness. This ambivalence is best represented by "uncertain terms".

17. E (Scope: *Whole Passage*)
The idea that the author is Inuit is implied in lines 40-43

18. E (Scope: *Whole Passage*)
Only choice (E) accurately captures the key components and groups of people in the passage: education, disagreement, parents, and educators.

19. B (Scope: *Lines 12-20*)
The idea of pragmatism is found in line 15 ("practical purpose"), while the idea of flexibility is found in lines 16-20.

20. B (Scope: *2nd Paragraph*)
According to the second paragraph, the school's education depends on matching students with perceived interests. This method assumes that the school can provide a forum for the student to pursue such an interest.

21. E (Scope: *3rd and 4th Paragraphs*)
The idea of cynicism can be found throughout the referenced paragraphs, but it is most concisely captured by the phrase "skeptical educators" (line 48).

22. C (Scope: *Line 52*)

The educators contend that all students should learn Math because alternative education limits "the potential achievements" (lines 49-50) of students. This argument depends on the assumption that all children need Math in order to succeed.

23. D (Scope: *Whole Passage*)

In the passage, the author simply relates facts in a tone that neither praises nor condemns the ideas. This neutral tone is best exemplified by the phrase "respectfully objective."

24. B (Scope: *Whole Passage*)

The dilemma, finding the best method of instruction, is in the first paragraph. Paragraphs two and three describe the possible solution of alternative education. The fourth and fifth paragraphs take a look at a contrary view of education.

OTHER TITLES AVAILABLE FROM FUSION PRESS

5 SAT Math Practice Tests

5 SAT Writing Practice Tests

10 SAT Vocabulary Practice Tests

Vocabulary Builder for ACT & SAT and Advanced TOEFL and SSAT

FORTHCOMING TITLES FROM FUSION PRESS

5 PSAT Math Practice Tests

5 PSAT Reading Practice Tests

5 PSAT Writing Practice Tests

10 PSAT Vocabulary Practice Tests

Score-Raising Vocabulary Builder for the GRE and GMAT